Ford

100 Years

Ford

100 Years

Mike Mueller

MOTORBOOKS
INTERNATIONAL

Commissioning Editor: MARIE CLAYTON
Editor: KATHERINE EDELSTON
Designer: PHILIP CLUCAS MSIAD
Reproduction: ANORAX IMAGING LTD
Printed & Bound in China

This edition published in 2003 by Motorbooks International, an imprint of MBI Publishing Company, Galtier Plaza, Suite 200, 380 Jackson Street, St. Paul, MN 55101-3885 USA

© Salamander Books Ltd., 2003

A member of **Chrysalis** Books plc

Motorbooks International titles are also available at discounts in bulk quantity for industrial or sales-promotional use. For details write to Special Sales Manager at Motorbooks International Wholesalers & Distributors, Galtier Plaza, Suite 200, 380 Jackson Street, St. Paul, MN 55101-3885 USA.

ISBN 0-7603-1580-9

Contents

Introduction

I t would take more than a few fingers and toes to count the car companies that have come and gone during the 100 years that Ford Motor Company has been in business. And it would require far more than a couple hundred pages to faithfully tell Ford's century-old tale. But we can only fit so much ink within these covers, so you'll just have to make do with this relatively "brief" overview. Or perhaps you can just look at the pictures.

Telling Henry Ford's personal story in itself would fill volumes, and has. His impact on American history can be measured in various ways, the least of which involves counting cars sold. Though he wasn't the first to build an automobile in Detroit, he was the man most responsible for popularizing the horseless carriage, and in doing so he mobilized America, he changed an entire way of life. Along with that, he also helped change the way American manufacturing worked, with the result being an even mightier U.S. presence on the international industrial front as other firms followed his lead.

But on the other side of the coin, he also helped redefine the term "stick in the mud." His refusal to change, to move onward and upward with the market that he himself put into rapid motion, quickly transformed a living legend into a tragic figure, an angry old man who refused to step aside and let fresher minds take over. Ford Motor Company might not have survived to see its 50th anniversary if not for the coming of a second World War and Henry's final capitulation—to his grandson, Henry Ford II. By the time Henry died in 1947, the company that bore his name was fortunately on the verge of a rebirth. And, as they say way too often, the rest is history.

Fifty-odd years later, Ford again is poised to make history. No, it's not the first car company to celebrate 100 years in business, but it's all the business that was done during those 10 decades that sets the Blue Oval apart from the others. Though General Motors loudly claims the biggest numbers in the automaking biz these days, no one has done it so well for so long as Ford. No one.

Here's to another hundred.

Mike Mueller
Kennesaw, Georgia, 2003

RIGHT: *Henry Ford's passion for the automobile was fired by his love of competition. A century separates these two racers that bear his name, seen at the 2002 Atlanta Auto Show.*

A Household Name Hits 100

"We use transverse springs for the same reason that we use round wheels," Ford snorted, "because we have found nothing better for the purpose."

One-hundred years? In many minds, it was no small wonder that Henry Ford's company had managed to make it to its 50th birthday in 1953. Old Henry had died six years before, and it was only three years prior to his death that he released the reins to the company that bore his name. As stubborn as the day is long right up to the end, it was his ingrained conservatism, coupled with his refusal to let cooler, clearer heads prevail that had very nearly cost everyone at Ford Motor Company their jobs. Who knows what would have happened had defense contract dollars not propped up the fading firm during the early 1940s.

How quickly the tables can turn. As late as 1925, Ford was still the world's leading automaker by leaps and bounds, and Henry was still more god than man. Other industrialists then looked to him for inspiration, and some parties even felt Mr. Ford and the White House would make a nice fit. But all that acclaim and admiration had dissipated within 10 years or so as both the boss and his company came back down to earth. Sure, the Great Depression did not help Ford's fortunes during the 1930s, but those trials and tribulations troubled all automakers, not just one. Hard times notwithstanding, General Motors began pulling away from Ford during that decade, basically because its leaders were willing to look to the future and Henry was not.

Granted, by the time World War II came along, the living legend who had brought us 15 million Model Ts and the moving assembly line had a good excuse—by that time he was nearly 80. He had suffered a stroke in 1938, and senility took over from there.

But was Henry really an old coot before this time? Many historians still shake their heads. Modern progress seemingly mattered so little to Detroit's big man, how could he have possible stayed so far ahead of the competition for so long?

The simple truth was that he did not. Chevrolet was hot on his heels by 1926, yet he still refused to update so many aging aspects of his increasingly antiquated products. Most often he would defend his obstinate stance by pointing out that simplicity was Ford's strongest selling point. It did not come much simpler than a transverse buggy spring, and that relic of the horseless carriage days amazingly still suspended Ford cars at both ends until 1949, only because Henry said so. He had continued saying so even after Chevrolet had introduced its innovative knee-action independent front suspension in 1934. "We use transverse springs for the same reason that we use round wheels," he snorted, "because we have found nothing better for the purpose."

Obviously superior modern advances like hydraulic brakes and Hotchkiss drive also

ABOVE: *The Model T Mark I (top) and the GT40 2003 (bottom) both demonstrate the unchanging Ford approach to automobile manufacture: they are as good as they can get, but they will get better.*

ABOVE: *Norman Rockwell bathes his nostalgic vision of Henry and Clara Ford in the workshop behind their house in a warm glow of domestic harmony. This may not be quite documentary in its accuracy.*

"When the second World War began, an increasingly paranoid Henry Ford figured that the whole affair was more or less part of a plot to help socialist-leaning Franklin Roosevelt take control of his company".

BELOW: *Henry Ford's products helped not only to make the country mobile but to make it fertile. Here he is assessing the performance of a 1917 Fordson tractor.*

failed to turn Henry's head. Chevrolet began installing hydraulic stoppers on its cars in 1935. Mechanical brakes continued offering Ford drivers "the safety of steel from toe to wheel" until 1939, again by the boss's iron-willed mandate. A Hotchkiss-type open driveshaft did not replace Ford's enclosed torque-tube drive until Dearborn's modern postwar models finally arrived in 1949. And, like the Model T it had powered for so many years, Ford's four-cylinder engine was also allowed to get a little long in the tooth before Henry finally allowed his engineers to introduce the fabled "flathead" V8 in 1932.

By then, Henry Ford's image had diminished considerably. Economic woes had led to violent labor strife at Ford barely 15 years after the boss had been lauded as a hero to the working man in honor of his ground-breaking $5-a-day wage. And the same man who had built schools and hospitals suddenly found himself the target of hated protests after he reportedly expressed his anti-Semitic beliefs. In 1938 he amazingly accepted an award from Adolph Hitler, which further alienated him from the Jewish community.

LEFT: *A Detroit Automobile Delivery Wagon from 1900–practicality from the outset.*

RIGHT: *Henry and Clara Ford with their grandson, Henry Ford II, along with the 1896 Quadricycle. This photograph was taken at Greenfield Village in 1945, the year that young Henry became president of the company.*

ABOVE: *This is thought to be the earliest existing photograph of Henry Ford, pictured behind the tiller of his Quadricycle, in Detroit, in 1896.*

Even his well-publicized anti-war sentiments were misleading to those who tried to determine what made this historic mover and shaker tick. Though he himself had protested loudly during the Great War of 1914-1918, he was not necessarily concerned with the tragic loss of life encountered by both sides during that bloody conflict. In his opinion, war was simply bad business, it was a waste of good working men, of valuable capital, of priceless time. When the second World War began, an increasingly paranoid Henry Ford figured that the whole affair was more or less part of a plot to help socialist-leaning Franklin Roosevelt take control of his company. Then Henry's only son (and the company's voice of reason) Edsel died in 1943, leaving behind a shaky house of cards that very easily could have folded soon afterwards if Henry Ford II had not stepped in to save the day.

Of course, to decline in status one has to have reached certain heights to begin with, and no one had risen so high, so fast during the 20th Century as Henry Ford. For all his eccentricities, the man had known something about the business of building cars, at least early on, and he had learned that business from the ground up.

"For 20 years Ford was the quintessential American automaker, thanks solely to the one man who wouldn't have had it any other way: Henry Ford."

Born on a Michigan farm on July 30, 1863, young Henry had grown up with "wheels in his head," as his father put it. Five years after marrying Clara Bryant in 1888, he had designed and built his first working internal combustion engine, and then followed that up with his first working automobile in 1896. Henry's Quadricycle took to the street of Detroit that summer, a few months after Charles Brady King had become the first to operate a horseless carriage in that city. Both men went on to long careers building automobiles, but only one became a household name.

RIGHT: *Seventy years of chassis development. Henry Ford raced "Old 999" on the ice at Lake St. Clair, near Detroit, in 1902. A replica is seen here with the 1972 Gran Torino Sport and its own stripped-down chassis and running gear.*

LEFT: *Henry Ford at the wheel of a 1903 Model A. Another Model A would debut in 1928, to follow the legendary Model T.*

ABOVE: *Edsel B. Ford II, pictured with the 1896 Quadricycle, the first motor vehicle produced by his great-grandfather's Ford Motor Company.*

Henry Ford's next step towards immortality came in July 1898 when, with the financial backing of Detroit mayor William Maybury and local investor William Murphy, he founded the Detroit Automobile Company, a firm that then foundered and was reorganized into the Henry Ford Company in November 1901. This second venture, too, failed to get off the ground, leading Murphy to bring in a consultant, Henry Leland, to help jump start things in March 1902. But the two Henrys clashed right off the bat, leading Ford to bail out. As part of his severance settlement, Henry Ford received $900 and the rights to his surname. Needing a new label, Leland's company then became Cadillac.

Henry Ford found another wealthy backer, the coal magnate Alexander Malcolmson, within a year, and on June 16, 1903, the two made history by establishing the Ford Motor Company. His outrageously successful Model T followed five years later, and there was nowhere to go but up from there. For 20 years Ford was the quintessential American automaker, thanks solely to the one man who would not have had it any other way: Henry Ford.

1896 Quadricycle

lara Ford knew all along that the many long hours her husband spent tinkering in the shed behind their house would eventually pay off. As Henry Ford later explained, "[i]t was a very great thing to have my wife even more confident than I was." Not only did Clara wholeheartedly trust Henry's abilities, she also never questioned his decisions, beginning in 1891 when he told the young farmer's daughter that they would be trading the quiet country life for the hustle and bustle of the city. Mr. Ford had found a job with the Edison Illuminating Company in Detroit, and Mrs. Ford obediently followed him there.

Clara also apparently never complained about Henry spending so much time back in that shed, even after their only son, Edsel, was born in November 1893. Two months later, Henry was promoted to Edison's chief engineer, but his main focus remained on his work at home. All those late nights and early mornings first resulted in the successful test of an operating gasoline engine on Christmas Eve that year. With an incredibly cooperative Clara dribbling fuel into the intake valve, Henry's small, one-cylinder, four-cycle creation sputtered to life right there in the Ford family's kitchen sink as Christmas dinner awaited attention. The phrase "behind every great man, there's a great woman" probably never rang so true.

Henry's devoted wife did not even begin to doubt his sanity when he took an axe to one of the shed's walls in June 1896. It seems he never thought about inventing the garage before he completed his first motorized carriage, which was too big to exit the small shop's equally small entrance. Ford did not build Detroit's

capable of speeds up to a dizzying 20 mph. It ran a few blocks up Bagley Avenue that early morning in 1896, died, was restarted, and puffed its way back home. Its jubilant driver then celebrated by taking a short nap before reporting to work at Edison on time, as usual.

By the summer of 1899, Henry Ford had built a second, more refined car, and he had also resigned his post at Edison to embark on his first automaking venture. As for the original Quadricycle, it was sold for $200 to help pay for the construction of that second machine. Fortunately it was later found and restored, and today is proudly displayed at the Henry Ford Museum.

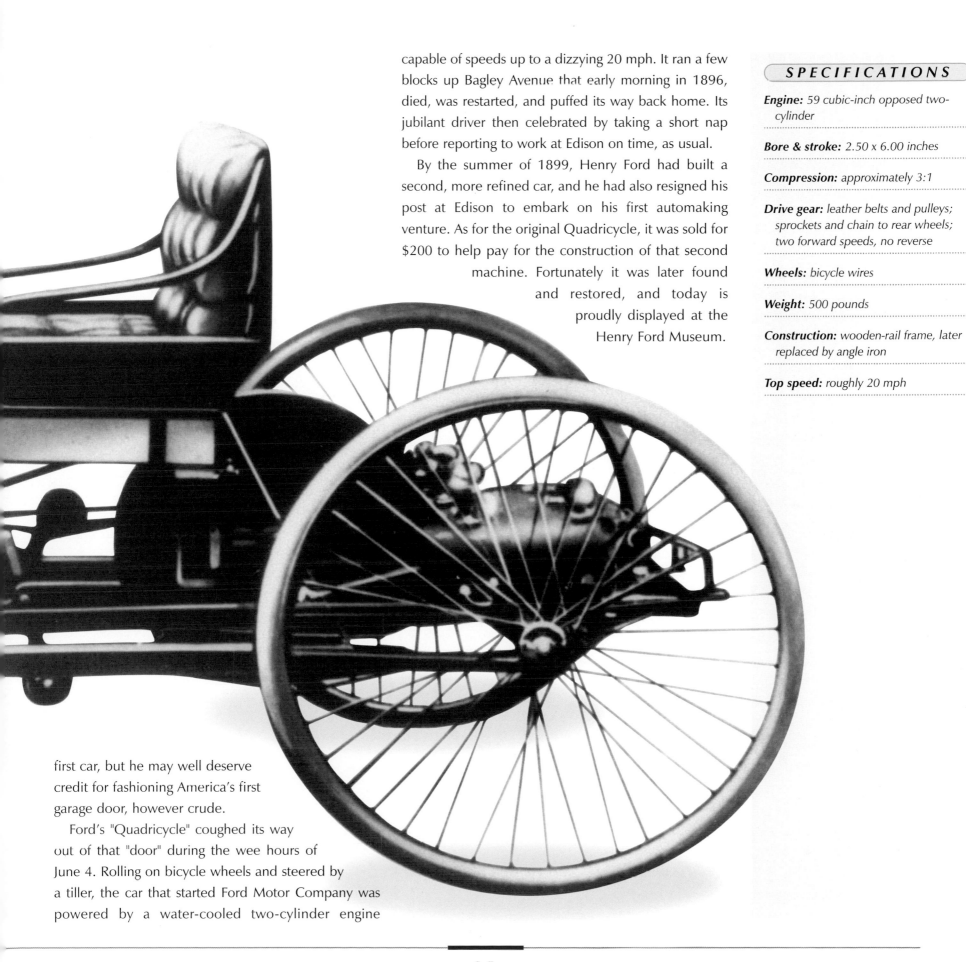

first car, but he may well deserve credit for fashioning America's first garage door, however crude.

Ford's "Quadricycle" coughed its way out of that "door" during the wee hours of June 4. Rolling on bicycle wheels and steered by a tiller, the car that started Ford Motor Company was powered by a water-cooled two-cylinder engine

SPECIFICATIONS

Engine: *59 cubic-inch opposed two-cylinder*

Bore & stroke: *2.50 x 6.00 inches*

Compression: *approximately 3:1*

Drive gear: *leather belts and pulleys; sprockets and chain to rear wheels; two forward speeds, no reverse*

Wheels: *bicycle wires*

Weight: *500 pounds*

Construction: *wooden-rail frame, later replaced by angle iron*

Top speed: *roughly 20 mph*

'999' Racer

The infernal internal-combustion engine had barely made its presence known in the horse-dominated world when the first competitive event pitting primitive automobile against primitive automobile was held. In November 1895, Hieronymous Mueller, of Decatur, Illinois, took his modified German-built Benz gasoline carriage north for a 50 mile jaunt from Chicago to Evanston and back, a run sponsored by the Chicago Times-Herald. This grueling test of man and machine, held long before heaters (let alone windshields) became optional equipment, was America's first officially sanctioned auto race. It ended with the Mueller-Benz, piloted by a nearly frozen Charles B. King, in second behind Charles Duryea's "buggyant."

Another pioneering automaker, Alexander Winton, then became the first big name in the motorsport game. In 1897, Winton clocked a mile in the then-sensational time of one minute, 48 seconds. He then used the resulting publicity to help promote his new autoworks, opened the following year. By 1899 the Winton company was America's third-best automotive venture, behind Locomobile and Columbia.

Winton's efforts served as inspiration for Henry Ford, who built his first race car in 1901. In October that year, Henry drove this speedster to a victory over Winton and his vaunted race car at Grosse Pointe, Michigan. His average speed for this event was 43.5 mph, heady stuff in those days.

Now a big name, too, Henry teamed up with bicycle racer Tom Cooper in early 1902 to build two more racers, both beastly bare-frame contraptions powered by enormous four-cylinder engines displacing 1,156 cubic inches.

"There was only one seat," he later explained. "One life to a car was enough. I tried out the cars. Cooper tried out the cars. We let them out at full speed. Going over Niagara Falls would have been but a pastime after a ride in one of them."

Neither partner wanted to risk racing their monsters, so Cooper enlisted another former bicycle racer, Barney Oldfield, who willingly took the two-handed tiller of the "999" car, named after a record-setting New York Central railroad locomotive. In October 1902, Oldfield opened up the 999 around the Grosse Pointe track and again beat Winton, this time soundly. Though he was no longer involved in the project, Henry Ford was right there at race's end to gather up the glory.

Early engine problems had convinced Henry to sell 999 to Cooper well before the 1902 Grosse Pointe race, but Tom apparently had no problem with his former partner taking advantage of the situation to gain even more fame. From there, Henry had nowhere to go but up.

As Benson Ford later explained in 1962, "at the turn of the century, my grandfather built the 'Old 999,' the world's first great racing car, and

raced it with the immortal Barney Oldfield at the tiller—performing miracles unheard of in its time. The publicity from his racing efforts attracted the capital that enabled him to create Ford Motor Company. It is interesting to speculate how history might have turned had it not been for the Old 999 and the fearless Barney Oldfield."

SPECIFICATIONS

Engine: 80-horsepower 1,156 cubic-inch four-cylinder

Bore & stroke: 7.25 x 7.00 inches

Wheelbase: 9 feet, four inches

Wheels: 34-inch wires, front; 36-inch wires, rear

Construction: bare-chassis race car; frame made of steel and white ash

Production: Henry Ford and Tom Cooper built two similar racers, "999" and "Arrow."

1903-10: Open for Business

"Many Americans remained unsure that the horseless carriage would catch on. But Henry Ford knew better, and he also recognized the key to the car's success from the outset: put the common man on motorized wheels and the horse would be put out to pasture posthaste."

ABOVE: *The fit and finish of the Model T—this is a 1909 Model, before compulsory black lacquer—was superb.*

Not many paid all that much attention when Ford Motor Company officially opened for business in June 1903. All three local Detroit newspapers failed to report the firm's historic founding until a few days after the fact. What was the hurry, anyway? Nearly 90 automobile manufacturing ventures sprung up that year around the country (only 15 of them in Michigan, by the way), nearly all of which hardly made a scratch in the history books. And with so many new shingles hanging about, total automobile production for 1903 still only amounted to barely 11,000. Many Americans even then remained unsure that the horseless carriage would catch on.

But Henry Ford knew better, and he also recognized the key to the car's success from the outset: put the common man on motorized wheels and the horse would be put out to pasture posthaste. This had been his plan at Detroit Automobile, and it remained his main goal after Alexander Malcomson came along to fund Ford Motor Company. Malcomson, however, had other ideas, as did company president (and Malcomson's uncle) John Gray.

While Ford's first car, the Model A, was a small, low-priced machine, it was soon overshadowed by bigger, more expensive offerings. The first Model A sold on July 15, 1903, and a steady stream followed, bringing instant success along with it. Capital funds had shrunk to nearly $200 in August. Then revenues soared to $37,000 within three months, all thanks to the Model A's appeal to the less-wealthy set. Henry's "$500 family car" was still a few years down the road, but he had to start somewhere. Why not at A?

Malcomson's influence began showing in 1904, when the Model B appeared with its big four-cylinder engine and hefty $2,000 asking price, followed thereafter by the pricier Model K and its even larger six-cylinder powerplant. Henry, meanwhile, remained focused on his original ideal, resulting in the introduction of the even-more-affordable Model N in 1906. Buoyed by Model N sales, Ford that year established itself as one of this country's top automakers. Clearly the man the company was named for was doing something right, but Malcomson's faction continued pushing for more prestigious luxury automobiles, cars Henry never did care for in the least.

The issue was finally settled about the time of Gray's death in July 1906. With the help of his ally, James Couzens, Henry Ford acquired controlling interest in the company that summer (buying out Malcomson along the way) then took over as president in October. He now had the final say, and that was bad news for the company's high-priced models. Though the costly Model K continued leading the way into 1908, it did not have long to live after word of an upcoming all-new car got out in March that year. Ford started in 1908 claiming four model lines; it ended with the

LEFT: *A 1909 Model T Touring model. The early body styles were "color-coded": red for tourers, grey for runabouts and green for town cars.*

company listing only one. Yet one was more than enough.

Henry's Model T milestone made it clear that both the horseless carriage and Ford Motor Company were here to stay. No longer merely playtoys for the rich, the automobile quickly found its way into the American mainstream, thanks entirely to the Tin Lizzie, and Ford immediately became the America's leading auto manufacturer in no uncertain terms.

"In 1913 Ford produced more than 168,000 Model Ts, and "America was suddenly on wheels," wrote *Automobile* magazine's David E. Davis, Jr., in 1996 while honoring "[t]he 24 Most Important Automobiles of the Century. By 1918, half of the cars on the entire planet were Ford Model Ts." The Boston News Bureau 70 years back had called that 1913 production total, "simply phenomenal"—this after claiming that

ABOVE: *The 1905 Model B was an elegant and expensive automobile, powered by a 24hp, 318 cu. ins. four, with a top speed of around 40mph.*

1912's run of 78,000 Ts was "remarkable."

Interesting to note as well was the fact that all those early Model Ts technically were "outlaws," as was every Ford automobile built up to that point. Henry Ford had failed to register his products with the industry's "proper authorities" back in 1903, though he had tried. He had approached that ruling body, the Association of Licensed Automobile Manufacturers, at least twice that year, but his license requests were turned down because ALAM officials among, other things, doubted the new company's ability to measure up to their group's "manufacturing standards."

The ALAM had been formed that same year basically to protect what was known as the "Selden patent." In 1895, George B. Selden had been granted U.S. patent rights to the "road carriage," this even though he had not then produced a working example like American automotive pioneers Charles and Frank Duryea had done two years before. Nonetheless, Selden was soon recognized as the rightful "keeper" of the gasoline-powered vehicle's design.

Henry won his case and took on the mantle of "giant-kille"... within a few years he would become "Goliath."

ABOVE: *Henry Ford at the wheel of a 1903 model A Runabout, the first product of the Ford Motor Company.*

ABOVE: *Introduced in 1907, the Model R featured a mechanical lubrication system that was a big improvement on the force-fed oiler of the Model N.*

In 1899 he assigned those rights to what would become the Electric Vehicle Company, of Hartford, Connecticut, after which time it was made perfectly clear that all American automaking ventures would have to pay homage to the Selden patent. More importantly, they would have to fork over a royalty of 1.25 per cent of their annual gross receipts or face legal action. By March 1903 most of this country's fledgling automotive firms had been strong-armed into accepting the situation as dictated. Some 25 of these companies then joined together to form the ALAM in the best interests of keeping the peace.

As much as Henry Ford preferred peace over the alternative, he was more than willing to square off with the Selden forces after he had initially agreed to pay their "ransom." If only they had just let Henry pay up. Instead, the group said he was not a viable venture; he then showed them by building Model As by the trainload. The group said he could not sell those unlicensed automobiles; he replied by continuing on unfazed. The group countered with a lawsuit in October 1903 claiming patent infringement; he swore in defiance that he would not give in, that he would not leave his customers flat.

The initial phase of the Ford-Selden court battle required four years to prepare, and then it was not until 1909 that the New York federal district court announced its ruling—in favor of Selden. Henry, of course appealed, claiming the patent was "a freak among alleged inventions."

Meanwhile he was becoming an American hero of sorts. The Detroit Free Press labeled him "Ford the Fighter." "There's a man for you, a man of backbone," proclaimed a *Free Press* editorial. "He presents a spectacle to win the applause of all men with red blood; for this world dearly loves the fighting man, and needs him, too, if we are to go forward."

As for Henry's fight, it moved on to the U.S. Court of Appeals, where it was won in January 1911. Although the court felt the Selden patent was viable, it found Ford not guilty of infringement, and the same ruling applied to other companies, too. It was a jubilant moment for all, especially so for Henry's firm, which reaped priceless public relations rewards in the wake of the legal victory. "No one factor publicized the company and its products as effectively as the company's role in liberating an industry," said Henry Ford later about his vindication in appeals court.

An overstatement perhaps? Overblown was more like it. The Model T had already publicized itself fairly effectively, and the company was certainly operating freely enough all along, showing no signs whatsoever of being shackled in any form or fashion by the Selden "monopoly." Production was flourishing even before the Model T came along to blow the lid of things in 1908. Penned in 1907, "Watch the Fords Go By" was not just a popular ad slogan, it was the way of the

RIGHT: 1905 Model C. The Model C was fitted with the 10hp version of the opposed twin-cylinder engine. The fuel tank was positioned under the hood.

BELOW: A Model T Mark I from 1909. By now—around car number 2500—the Model T had become pretty much standardized. Windshields and tops were still opional, as were the gas headlamps.

Meanwhile Ford was becoming an American hero of sorts. The Detroit Free Press labeled him "Ford the Fighter." "There's a man for you, a man of backbone," proclaimed a Free Press editorial. "He presents a spectacle to win the applause of all men with red blood; for this world dearly loves the fighting man, and needs him, too, if we are to go forward."

automotive world for many years to come. By the time Henry had won his case and taken on the mantle of "giant-killer," it was he who stood on the verge of monopolizing the industry. Within a few years he would become "Goliath."

Equally gigantic was the new building that was then turning out Model T's at unheard-of rates. Opened almost one year exactly before the Selden case was finalized, Ford's massive Highland Park plant was a wonderment known around the world, and a far cry from the humble surroundings that had been home to the company just seven years before. The original Mack Avenue plant in Detroit, destroyed by fire many years ago, was a wagon shop converted into an automobile-production facility. It stood up under the strain of success for only two years. In 1905 Ford moved to new works on Piquette Avenue, a facility that was 10 times larger than the former "plant." The Model T's arrival then forced Henry Ford to look for even larger premises.

Built in Highland Park, a suburb surrounded by the city of Detroit, Henry's next assembly complex was designed by local celebrity Albert Kahn, then this country's most famed industrial architect. As aesthetically pleasing as it was enormous, the new plant at the time represented both the world's largest car factory and the biggest thing under one roof in Michigan. The modern-looking four-story complex measured 865 feet long and 75 feet wide and incorporated 50,000 square feet of glass, leading to it being nicknamed the "Crystal Palace."

Almost immediately roughly 16,000 workers called the Crystal Palace home, and about 12,000 of those people posed in front of the building for a publicity photo that showed up in many newspapers in 1905. According to publicists, that image represented "the largest specially posed photo ever taken and [is] far and away the most expensive, considering the employees' time and loss of production."

It was also the last time anyone was caught standing around at Ford Motor Company.

1903 Model A

Ford Motor Company history began, appropriately enough, with the aptly named Model A. Introduced in July 1903, Ford's original Model A was a two-seat Runabout priced at $850. Henry had hoped to offer a $500 car, but reality prevailed. He also wanted to keep weight down at all costs, and in this he succeeded, tipping the scales at a scant 1,250 pounds.

Like so many early American automobiles, the Model A mounted its steering wheel on the right, European-style. Power came from an opposed two-cylinder that sent eight honest horsepower to the rear wheels via chain drive. Those wheels were tall wooden spokes shod in 28 x 3 inch clincher tires. Up top, there was no protection from weather for the driver and passenger, but there was the optional tonneau bodywork that added seating for two more riders in the back. The tonneau's price was $100. An optional top, priced at $50, was introduced for the 1904 Model A.

The Model A was Ford's sole product up until September 1904,

when both the Model C and Model AC debuted, still as 1904 models. The Model C looked less like a horseless carriage and more like an automobile thanks to its hooded front end, beneath which was the company's larger, more powerful two-cylinder. The Model C's 10-horsepower engine remained located beneath the seat. The AC was a lengthened Model A fitted with the Model C's bigger motor.

Production figures for those early years vary as confusion exists concerning model breakdowns. Some early sources put total Model A production for 1903 and 1904 combined at 1,708 but a more believable total eventually surfaced at 670. Reportedly that 1,708 figure referred to all models built up to September 30, 1904, so a lesser number for the Model A is then only logical.

Whatever the case, a survey in 1978 determined that 82 Model A Fords still existed worldwide by then. Today, one of these pioneers can be found at the Henry Ford Museum.

1906 Model K

The last year for two-cylinder models from Ford was 1906. On the other side of the coin, it was the first year for two new models; one that foretold the future, another that represented a dead end. The former, the Model N, was a low-priced, two-passenger Runabout with a front-mounted four-cylinder engine. Called "distinctly the most important mechanical traction event of 1906" by *Cycle and Automobile Trade Journal*, the $600 Model N laid the groundwork for an even greater event to come near the end of 1908.

The latter, the Model K, which was introduced late in 1905, was as far away from Henry Ford's ideal for a "car for the multitudes" as was possible. Available either as a touring car or Runabout, the Model K was powered by Ford's first six-cylinder engine, a huge chunk of iron that could reportedly propel the Runabout to 60 mph—heady stuff for 1906. The powerful and somewhat posh (for a Ford) Model K was priced at $2,500, five times what Henry thought his company's products should cost. And after 1906, it was Mr. Ford's opinion that mattered most. Make that entirely.

Though the relatively ostentatious Model K remained in production into 1908, it did not have long to live after Henry Ford completed work on the car he had wanted all along. The Model K, along with all other existing Ford models, was deleted in October that year in favor of a historic milestone that salted away the Ford moniker as a household name: the Model T.

SPECIFICATIONS

Engine: *40-horsepower 405 cubic-inch inline six-cylinder*

Bore & stroke: *4.25 x 4.25 inches*

Fuel delivery: *Holley updraft carburetor*

Transmission: *two-speed planetary gearbox*

Brakes: *rear-wheel mechanical, lever operated*

Price: *$2,500*

Wheelbase: *114 or 120 inches*

Weight: *2,400 pounds*

Model availability: *four-passenger, two-door touring car and four-passenger, two-door Runabout*

Construction: *body on frame*

Production: *not available*

1909 Model T

The official model-year designation for Ford's first Model T remains debatable to this day. Introduced in October 1908, the original "Tin Lizzie" was undoubtedly intended to be a "1909" offering. But all the hype expended during that initial year forever branded the earliest Ts with a calendar-correct "1908" label. About 300 Model Ts were built (other sources say as few as 126) at the Piquette Avenue plant before January 1, 1909, after which time the point was rendered moot. Historically speaking, 1908 was obviously the first year for Henry's "universal car," and that is the reference used commonly by historians.

Whichever date you prefer, the historic aspects of the original Model T do not change one iota: it is the most significant automobile ever built, certainly by U.S. standards, arguably from a worldwide perspective. Its affordable simplicity helped put America on wheels—and Dearborn on the automaking map. In boldface. Ford was already a pioneer in his field by 1908, but buoyed by runaway Model T sales, Henry's company quickly became far and away the industry leader.

By 1911 Ford's annual profits had grown to an amount greater than those of all other American automobile manufacturers combined that year. A similar comparison could have been made concerning production figures in 1913, the year Ford built more than 200,000 cars for the first time. The company simply had not been able to keep up with demand in 1908 and 1909, when more than 10,000 Model Ts rolled off the line. Fifteen years later, annual production had soared to two million, and it was only then that rivals—specifically Chevrolet—finally started reeling Detroit's

runaway sales champ back in.

There probably exists no other greater example of the "don't fix it if it ain't broke" ideal. Henry just might have continued building Model Ts for another 15 years if Chevrolet had not come out of virtually nowhere to eventually upset his apple cart in the late 1920s. But by 1924—the year the 10 millionth Model T found a home—the situation had become painfully obvious: Ford's main attraction was not necessarily broken, it simply was no longer capable of staying ahead of the new Chevrolets. Reportedly Ernest Kanzler, one of Ford's vice presidents

and Henry's brother-in-law, then sent a carefully worded letter to Henry suggesting a change was in order. Though Kanzler's letter was right on the mark, he still lost his job for his perceived impertinence. If only hard-headed old Henry could have fired everyone over at Chevrolet while he was at it.

But not even Henry Ford's iron will could stop the inevitable. Chevrolet surely would have caught up with Ford soon enough but it did so a few years earlier than expected after Henry closed his shop down completely in May 1927 to prepare for the introduction of his first all-new offering in nearly 20 years: the Model A.

Ford built its last Model T on May 26, 1927, after 15 million had been sold. It took almost 50 years for another affordable small car, the VW Beetle, to break that all-time sales record.

SPECIFICATIONS

Engine: *20-horsepower 176 cubic-inch L-head inline four-cylinder with separate cylinder block and head.*

Bore & stroke: *3.75 x 400 inches*

Compression: *4.5:1*

Transmission: *two-speed planetary unit with foot-pedal controls*

Steering: *wheel located on lefthand side, popularizing a trend that would then proliferate throughout the American market*

Suspension: *transverse buggy springs and solid axles, front and rear*

Brakes: *hand-operated mechanical units for rear wheels only; foot-activated contracting bands on driveshaft*

Price: *began at $850*

Wheelbase: *100 inches*

Weight: *1,200 pounds for the first touring cars.*

Model availability: *a touring car and three-passenger runabout appeared early on; these were joined later in 1909 by a Landaulet, a Town Car and a rare closed sedan*

Construction: *body on frame (bodies were wood panels over wood frames; fenders were stamped steel)*

Production: *approximately 10,000*

1911-20: Massive Marketing

"Simply put, Henry Ford turned mass production into massive production with a moving assembly line system that worked better and faster than anything seen before. Be it wax candles or widgets, no product had ever been turned out at the dizzying rates being demonstrated at Highland Park by 1914."

Witnesses from around the world continued to marvel over Ford's Highland Park plant for many years after its grandiose opening in January 1910. Such was the demand to see the Crystal Palace that tours were even organized that year. By early 1914, as many as 150 people a day were being shown around the massive facility. Some 100,000 visited the works in 1915, and within two years the number of annual visitors had doubled again.

Included in these numbers was everyone from president William Howard Taft to the "Average Joe." Rival automakers, from the U.S. and overseas, were also eager to see what made Ford Motor Company tick so well, and all came away from their visits impressed. "The Ford plant is the most remarkable in the world," said Benz general manager Karl Neumaier, "It is the very best in equipment and method."

It was also the world's busiest. Production in 1910 increased by 50 per cent from 1909, and by 1911 production had nearly doubled again; increases that both amazed rivals and taxed even the limits of the expansive, highly advanced Highland Park plant.

To relieve the pressure on Highland Park and cut overall costs, Henry opened his first branch plant in 1911. Located in Kansas City, this facility was built to clean up—in Henry's words—"the wasteful inefficiency in freighting fully-assembled cars in quantity to distances several thousand miles from Detroit." By 1915 Ford had 25 branch assembly operations across the country, all overseen by production manager William S. Knudsen, the mover and shaker who would later lead Chevrolet past Ford in the sales race. Ford also opened his first overseas plant in 1911, near Manchester, England.

Wasteful inefficiency was also addressed in the basic assembly process itself. Cadillac's Henry Leland had originated the idea of interchangeable parts between different models to cut costs, save space and minimize assembly hassles. Ransom Olds was among the first (if not the first) to use a moving production line, explaining why Oldsmobile was briefly America's top automaker. Ford then took it from there, combining and refining, making his own innovative inputs, until he made industrial manufacturing history.

Ford began operating its moving assembly line in April 1913, then put it into full-time use in January the following year. Historic repercussions were immediate.

ABOVE: *Before World War I, Model Ts were fitted with gas headlamps - hence the cylinder on the running board. Ford threatened that the fitting of any non-standard accessories would nullify the warranty.*

ABOVE: *This cutaway of a Fordson tractor shows the simplicity of the power train.*

ABOVE: *Gasoline was used to start and warm up the engine of the Fordson, a machine that was best remembered not just for its technical advances but that its affordability persuaded thousands of small farmers to take the plunge and buy their first tractor.*

Calendar-year output went from 78,400 in 1912 to 168,200 in 1913, and that was just the beginning. By 1915, Ford was building more than 500,000 Model Ts a year, leading to rapid-fire production milestones that continued to amaze the world. Highland Park rolled out Model T number one million in December 1915, three months after the one millionth Ford built since 1903 had hit the streets. The two millionth Model T then came in June 1917, followed by the three millionth in April 1919, and the four millionth in May 1920.

Simply put, Henry Ford turned mass production into massive production with a moving assembly line system that worked better and faster than anything seen before, in any line of work. Be it wax candles or widgets, no product had ever been turned out at the dizzying rates being demonstrated at Highland Park by 1914. In perfecting the assembly line, Henry radically reduced the time required to build a Model T—from 14 man hours per car in early 1913, to one-and-a-half hours by October that year. In 1914 the Highland Park plant began rolling 1,000 Model Ts a day off the line.

Production moved so fast that workers could not wait for the slow-drying paints of the day to dry, meaning Ford had to rely on a certain kind of relatively fast-drying

"When you see [Ford's] modest little car running by, take your hat off."

THE EAST BOSTON FREE PRESS.

enamel that came in only one shade. And thus, in turn, came the now famous quote: "you can have any color you want, as long as it's black." Beginning in 1914 all Model Ts were black, and they would remain so until 1925. But making a plain car even plainer did nothing to curb customer enthusiasm, which continued to grow every year.

In the meantime, prices had gone down, per the boss's unwavering mandate, as production costs dropped like a rock. A basic Model T Runabout's bottom line was $900 in 1910, $680 in 1911, $512 in 1913, $440 in 1915, and $345 in 1917. Affordability had never come so cheap, and yet Ford Motor Company profits were running through the roof. According to Henry, his company attracted 1,000 new customers for every dollar he snipped off a price tag, and for every new customer Ford's top people grew ever more wealthy.

The idea then came to Henry to spread that wealth around even further. Company executives were making big bucks by 1914, but what about workers down on the assembly line? In January that year Ford gave his plant people a raise from $2.34 a day to an amazing $5 per shift. And at the same time he reduced the work day from 10 hours to 8, which in turn meant that daily shifts were expanded from two to three to keep up the company's prodigious production pace.

Henry's "five-dollar workday" rocked the world unlike anything else he had done to date and was still big news many decades down the road. Forty years after the fact, the *London Economist* recalled it as "the most dramatic event in the history of wages."

ABOVE: *Henry Ford's first love had been race cars and his production cars were used in competition from the earliest days as this stripped-down, 1915 model shows.*

"I consider that what Henry Ford accomplished in 1914 contributed far more to the emancipation of workers than the [Russian] Revolution of 1917," claimed French intellectual R.L. Bruckberger in 1959, "He took the worker out of the class of the 'wage-earning proletariat' to which Marx had relegated him and made every worker a potential customer."

ABOVE: *The Model T was infinitely adaptable to the specific requirements of the customer...*

Back in 1914, the *New York Herald* referred to Henry's wage hike as "an epoch in the world's industrial history." "When you see [Ford's] modest little car running by, take your hat off," added the *East Boston Free Press*. According to the *Cleveland Plain Dealer*, the five-dollar workday announcement "shot like a blinding rocket through the dark clouds of the present industrial depression." Indeed, the entire world was mired in an economic slump as "The Great War" neared, making Henry's generous move even more amazing.

Of course, Henry Ford was so generous then because he could afford to be with

ABOVE: *This Mark I Model T of 1911 shows the restyled fenders and radiator. Revisions were also made to the motor and axles.*

ABOVE: *This 1917 Model T demonstrates beautifully how the Ford had become part of the American landscape.*

RIGHT: *Another Mark II from 1917, in standard trim. By now all the brasswork had been removed, giving the car an altogether more workmanlike aspect.*

ease. And he was additionally well aware of the move's priceless public relations value, as well as what it would do for employee morale. Compassion for his workforce perhaps came into play somewhere in there.

In 1915 Henry's anti-war sentiments came to the fore when he sponsored the "Peace Ship" mission. But this group of politicians, businessmen and such could not even keep the peace amongst themselves during their cruise across the Atlantic. Not only did the mission fail miserably, it also led to financial manager James Couzens' resignation after clashes with Henry over his pacifist politics.

On top of that, Henry also brought a suit against the *Chicago Tribune* in 1916, claiming libel after the paper had labeled him an anarchist following the "Peace Ship" debacle. Ford finally won the suit in 1919.

Yet another lawsuit had taken Henry into court in November 1916 after he announced that he would suspend special dividend payments to stockholders, choosing instead to invest that cash back into the company. Major stockholders John and Horace Dodge sued Ford for $25 million and won three years later. During the case, Henry's distaste for the stockholding structure grew, the result of his belief that people who did nothing to produce a product, nothing to earn their dividends, should not receive moneys that rightfully belonged to a company and its workers.

A clever, downright conniving plan rid him of these "parasites" in 1919. The ploy began with his resignation from the company president's office on December 30, 1918, after which his son Edsel was named his successor. Henry then started rumors that he was planning to open a new business to build a car that would undersell the Model T. When newspapers began reporting these rumors as fact, stockholders and dealers panicked. Henry's agents swept in and bought up all the company stock, a maneuver that was completed by July 1919 at a cost of $105 million. Presto! The Ford family was then 100 per cent in control of the company that bore their name.

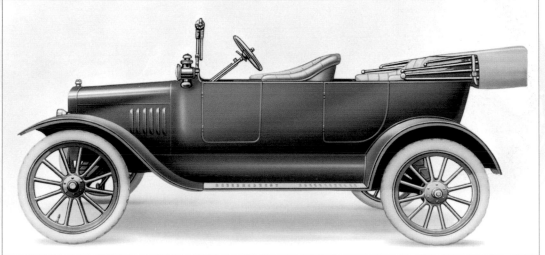

1911 Model T Torpedo Runabout

Just because Ford built the Model T for nearly two decades did not mean buyers got the same old car every year. There were many improvements along the way, including new bodystyles, two of which appeared in 1911: an open Runabout and the Torpedo Runabout. Actually introduced in October 1910, these two sporty "Flivvers" are often referred to as 1910 models, but grouping them along with 1911's many other attractive updates only seems right.

New that year were bodies made of sheet steel over wood framing, construction that truly inspired the "Tin Lizzie" nickname. Fenders were distinctively restyled and axles were beefed up front and rear. The four-cylinder's valve springs were now covered by a protective plate, while access openings were incorporated into the crankcase and the transmission housing to allow easier maintenance on both the bearings and drive bands.

Easily the sharpest-looking Model T yet, the Torpedo Runabout was Ford's first roadster to feature doors. The open Runabout was simply a Torpedo roadster without the doors and accompanying body panels. In both cases, sporty impressions resulted from a bit of lowering. With the same 100-inch wheelbase as other Model Ts, the seats were mounted lower and farther back than in typical 1911 Ts. Bodywork too was

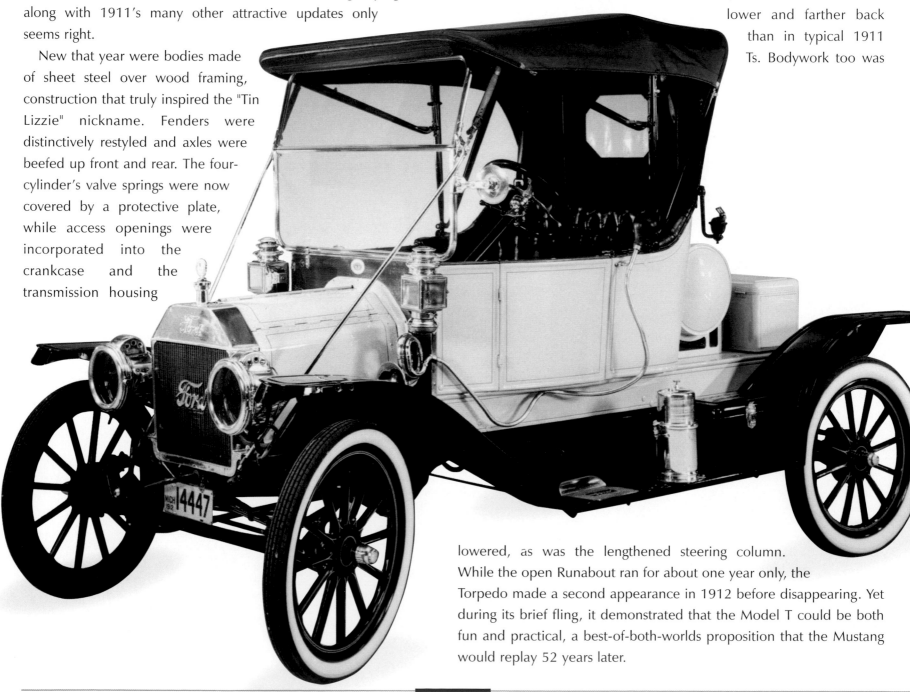

lowered, as was the lengthened steering column. While the open Runabout ran for about one year only, the Torpedo made a second appearance in 1912 before disappearing. Yet during its brief fling, it demonstrated that the Model T could be both fun and practical, a best-of-both-worlds proposition that the Mustang would replay 52 years later.

1915 Model T Sedan

Two modernized Model Ts were introduced late in 1914, as 1915 models. One was the Coupelet, Dearborn's first true convertible, which had real side glass and a folding top, although door windows still had to be raised and lowered by hand.

The other was Ford's first "modern" closed car, a two-door sedan. While closed Model T bodies had been offered before, they were gawky, old-fashioned "phone-booth-looking," concoctions of wood. These termite traps were highly unpopular as consumer trends still favored open cars because of both cost and personal taste. Closing up an automobile was a compromise; having the wind in the hair and bugs in the teeth were part of the internal-combustion experience, or at least that was true before World War I.

Closed cars became more popular once automobile use became widespread and manufacturers found better, cheaper ways to build effective, affordable all-weather bodies. Ford's first steel-shelled sedan emerged as the least popular Model T in 1915. But it was not long before Flivver buyers realized that they did not have to be uncomfortable while travelling from A to B, a trip that grew increasingly annoying in open cars as road speeds increased.

Engine: 176.7 cubic-inch L-head inline four-cylinder

Transmission: two-speed planetary unit controlled by three pedals and one lever

Brakes: hand operated mechanical units for rear wheels only; foot-activated contracting bands in transmission

Price: $975 early on; $750 by the summer of 1915

Wheelbase: 100 inches

Weight: 1,730 pounds

Model availability: two-door, five-passenger, full-bodied sedan

Construction: body on frame; steel panels over wood framing with glass side windows

Production: 989 (for fiscal year August1, 1915 to July 30, 1916)

1917 Model TT 1-ton Truck

Though it has not yet been running for 100 years, Ford's truck legacy still ranks as Detroit's oldest, but not by much. The Big Three all jumped up on the commercial vehicle bandwagon in rapid fashion, one after the other right about the time World War I was coming to an end. The last of the trio to get going, Chevrolet, quickly climbed to the top of the heap during the 1930s and stayed there until the 1970s. Dodge trucks have always run a distant third, although they have closed that gap considerably within the last 15 years or so.

But in the beginning it was Ford that far and away dominated the Big Three truck race—this even though old Henry apparently did not care about hard-working haulers early on. No, he was not blind to an opportunity to sell more vehicles. In fact, an enclosed delivery wagon was the first model rolled out by his Detroit Automobile Company in January 1900. And two years after the Ford Motor Company was founded, he was again testing the commercial vehicle waters, this time with the "Model C fitted with our Delivery Top." Only 10 or so were built, however, and his next "truck" did not come along for another seven years.

This time the goal was to build a better beast of burden, resulting in what Ford called "The Car That Delivers The Goods." Not just a lightly modified automobile, this new breed featured a unique panel-truck body and was "tougher than an army of mules and cheaper than a team of horses." Nonetheless, it too failed to deliver the customers and was cancelled in January 1912.

While various other Ford trucks had started showing up for work about then, all were aftermarket conversions. More than one independent business had emerged by 1913 to offer buyers the opportunity to transform their Ford car into a truck. Most prominent perhaps was A. D. Smith, which offered the Smith Form-a-Truck conversion. The parts included in this deal turned a polite

Model T into a lengthened, chain-driven one-ton workhorse. Panel truck conversion kits also became popular just prior to World War I.

Then apparently Henry finally grew tired of seeing outside firms profiting from his products. On July 27, 1917, Dearborn officials announced the availability of Ford's first true truck, the Model TT one-ton chassis. This was still a modified passenger-car platform, but it nonetheless offered rugged qualities that only a truck could. The Model

TT's reinforced frame featured a wheelbase measuring two feet longer than the Model T's. Suspension in the back was beefed up and a tougher worm-drive rear axle was installed, as were artillery-type rear wheels wearing solid rubber tires. All that added toughness made the Model TT an overnight success. Ford would sell 100,000 one-ton chassis trucks by 1919.

Yet Henry continued to let other businessmen slip their hands into his pockets. Bare-chassis Ford trucks remained the only choices into the 1920s. Adding cabs and beds was still left up to the customer, at least until Ford noticed that both Dodge and Chevrolet had started building trucks. Still an independent (it was later purchased by Walter Chrysler in 1928), the Dodge Brothers firm had rolled out its new "commercial car" in October 1917, while the first Chevy trucks showed up early in 1918 in both half- and one-ton forms.

To stay ahead of these two young rivals, Ford began offering bodywork for its Model TT one-ton chassis in October 1923. First came a pickup-style body, which actually came about through a collaborative effort between Ford's Highland Park plant, the Budd body company in Philadelphia and Simplex Manufacturing in Kansas City, Missouri. Ford's first fully "factory-built" body, an open C-cab, appeared in January 1924. An eight-foot stake bed appeared later in December, followed by an enclosed cab in the spring of 1925.

Model TT truck production soared to 250,000 that year. Another 228,000 followed in 1926, by which time Ford reportedly claimed 75 per cent of the truck market, a feat no firm has come close to matching since—not even Chevrolet during its highly successful 30-year run at the top. Today it is Ford trucks that have been leading their Chevrolet rivals around by the nose for roughly 30 years. And to think it all began with a rude, crude, bare-chassis bruiser back in 1917.

SPECIFICATIONS

Engine: *20-horsepower 176.7 cubic-inch L-head four-cylinder*

Price: *$625*

Wheelbase: *124 inches*

Weight: *1,450 pounds*

Model availability: *bare-chassis one-ton truck (adding bodywork was left up to customer)*

1917 Fordson Tractor

Henry Ford grew up in farm country outside Dearborn, but he never liked farming. He preferred machines, and it was the creation of labor-saving farm equipment that initially captured his imagination, though he practically dropped work on the tractor until the automobile was in production. He resumed work in late 1905. Prototype tractors were up and working by 1907, but his board of directors never gave approval for production. The project was shelved until July 1917 when Henry Ford & Son, was founded to build what became known as the "Fordson" tractor.

Ford's experiments with Model T "tractors" had dated back to 1915, and various independent companies had created similar conversion kits before the Fordson was introduced to the U.S. in

October 1917, while special high-priority wartime production for a desperate British agriculture had been going on since December 1916. During the tractor's first three months in the U.S. 5,000 Fordsons were delivered. By July 1918, the Brady Street plant in Dearborn was spitting out 131 tractors a day. Three years later, Henry Ford could claim control of two-thirds of America's tractor market.

Then the competition responded. International Harvester's general-purpose Farmall appeared in 1924, after which Fordson demand began to slide. Ford stopped selling tractors in the U.S. in 1928 after more than 750,000 Fordsons had been built, but then restarted production in 1939 with the 9N, followed by the 2N in 1942, and the 8N in 1948. During his lifetime Henry watched 1.7 million tractors leave his plants.

1919 'Self-Starting' Model T

In the beginning cars required a strong arm to bring them to life, and woe to the driver who let one of those hand cranks kick back on him. Bruises and broken bones were not uncommon before Cadillac introduced its electric "self-starter" in 1912. Cranks remained an American staple throughout the 1920s, but electric starter motors became all the rage once they filtered down to the low-priced ranks.

Ford's first electric starter appeared in 1919 as a $75 option, but only for closed Model Ts. It became a standard feature on coupes and sedans by mid-1919, at which time open Ts began showing up with the new system, once again as a $75 option. A $25 demountable rim, also debuted in 1919, making flat tires less trouble. Along with an ultra-convenient starter motor, the electrical system included a storage battery, a generator, and head- and taillights. In order to mount these extras and allow them to operate, the engine block and transmission case had to be redesigned. A ring gear was added to the flywheel to give the starter something to start, and a stronger timing gear went onto the camshaft to serve as a drive source for the six-volt generator. Ignition chores remained a flywheel-fired magneto's responsibility, as it would throughout the Model T's life.

Model Ts built later in 1919 received the updated engine block and transmission case, once stores of the old castings ran out. By 1927 all Fords built featured convenient demountable rims and electric starters.

1921-30:
One Step Forward, One Step Back

BELOW: *Ford's total production had passed the 10 million mark in 1924, 21 years years after the first Model A had rolled off the Dearborn line. From then on, production of the model T would regularly exceed a million cars a year. By the time Model T production officially ceased in 1927, over 15 million Fords had been built.*

RIGHT: *Elegance as well as utility could be provided under the Ford banner, witnessed by this splendid Lincoln Sedanca of 1922.*

The 1920s began on a downer for Ford, even though the firm remained far and away the leader of America's automotive pack. A national recession arrived in 1920 to help turn back Model T sales that year to nearly 50 per cent of 1919's total, resulting in a corresponding precipitous drop in market share from 49 per cent down to 22. America's economic woes then continued through the winter into 1921 leaving no apparent relief in sight.

Any other automaker might have been worried, but not Henry Ford. In September 1920 he cut his prices yet again—this time by the greatest margins in industry history—forcing the competition into a frenzy. Some rivals complained of unfair business practices. Others obstinately stood by and did nothing. But many also dropped their prices accordingly, but with nowhere near the same results seen at Ford.

Within a few months Henry followed his price-slashing up by basically shoving his leftover Model T surplus down dealer's throats in February 1921, this after all plants had sat "closed for inventory" during January. Per the practices of the day, those dealers either had to pay up or close up, so it was left to them to beg the required cash from their bankers. That "ransom money" then gave Ford the breathing room he needed without making his own trip to the lender's office along an already well-worn path. "Humanitarian Henry?" Who was kidding whom?

Fortunately demand quickly restarted in the spring of 1921, so dealers too got out of hot water in short order. As for Henry, he was once again watching the Fords go by at record paces. Production went back on a meteoric rise, and by the end of the year the company's annual market share hit an unworldly 61.5 per cent. That was followed in 1922 by more than one million Model Ts, a new all-time high and the industry's first yearly total to run into the then-unimagined seven-digit range.

ABOVE: *From its introduction in 1908 to the last car built in 1927, only the Model T's price.was radically revised, the 176.7 cubic inch L-Head remained unchanged.*

"In September 1920 Henry Ford simply cut his prices yet again—this time by the greatest margins in industry history—forcing the competition into a frenzy."

Ford's six millionth Model T appeared in May 1922, almost one year exactly after the 5 millionth had left the line in 1921. Henry's 10 millionth rolled out in 1924, and another 5 million were built before the Model T was finally discontinued in May 1927.

Henry Ford had mortgaged the world to pay off his 1916 stockholder buy-out and spent a fortune building his colossal River Rouge complex south of Detroit, yet he was still able to remain on top despite economic hard times. Constructed on 1,000 acres along the Rouge River in 1915, Ford's new industrial complex eventually displaced the Highland Park plant as the world's largest manufacturing facility. World War I temporarily interrupted Rouge construction, but the works were shaping up famously by 1919, as were Henry's plans to make his company as self-sufficient as possible. To that end, River Rouge included a deep-water port that allowed Great Lakes freighters to bring in raw materials directly from their sources. On its grounds were coke ovens,

BELOW: *The last of the line: a pristine, 1927 Model T Roadster.in standard trim - without bumpers, which were, to the end, an option, at $15 extra.*

RIGHT: *Production of the Model T truck chassis ran on for a while after the car was replaced by the model A. 228,496 were produced in 1926.*

ABOVE: *The two door pick-up version of the Model T remained popular throughout 1926 and 1926. Over 75,000 were sold in the final year..*

blast furnaces and a powerplant, as well as body-building and assembly facilities. American industry had never seen anything like it before, but what else would you expect from Henry Ford? Certainly not additional expansion involving production of a new luxury-car line. Yet that is what happened in February 1922 when Ford purchased the Lincoln Motor Company, founded by Henry's old nemesis, Henry Leland, in 1920. Under Edsel Ford's artistic direction, Lincoln would later rise up with the cream of America's fine-car crop. But during the 1920s, Henry's luxury division more or less rode the coattails of its record-breaking corporate cousin.

Additional corporate expansion included Ford's first true engineering center, which broke ground in Dearborn in 1923 and was dedicated in January 1925. Other assembly facilities continued to sprout around the world, and by 1926 Ford was operating 60 plants in America, together with 28 overseas. Henry even brightened things up around the assembly lines that year by reintroducing color choices for the Model T.

But not all was so rosy around Henry's office during the decade's first half. He invited a boycott of his cars after a series of anti-Semitic articles were published in Ford's weekly magazine, the *Dearborn Independent*, in 1920. How much this boycott contributed to the company's sales decline that year is anyone's guess, though most industry-watchers figured it made little impact.

Then a second smear campaign started up in the magazine in 1924, and this time Henry Ford was sued for defamation of character. After settling this suit out of court in July 1927, Henry ran both a personal apology and a formal retraction of all prior offensive statements, which greatly eased the situation. But Ford later re-opened old wounds in 1938 by allowing Adolph Hitler to bestow him with the Grand Cross of the

ABOVE: *During 1924 closed cars, like this Fordor sedan, got all-steel bodies, replacing the wood frame construction of earlier models.*

RIGHT: *This late Model T sports a number of optional extras, including bumpers, wire wheels and headlamps.*

ABOVE: *This Lincoln Model L, Deitrich Coupe Roadster of 1926 epitomizes "Roaring Twenties" Style.*

"Ford later re-opened old wounds by allowing Hitler to bestow him with the Grand Cross of the Supreme Order of the German Eagle, the Third Reich's highest honor for a foreigner."

Supreme Order of the German Eagle, the Third Reich's highest honor for a foreigner. Another boycott followed, and this time Jewish-Americans were not the only ones offended as the world spun all but out of control towards a second global conflict.

Another blow fell in January 1924, when William Knudsen took his talents over to General Motors, where he became president and general manager at Chevrolet, where he expected Chevy to catch up with Ford in the industry sales race. Within three years Chevrolet had passed its rival on the sales charts. Henry's hesitance to replace the aging Model T with something more modern helped open a door for GM's low-priced division to storm right through. Despite ever-strong sales, the handwriting had started appearing on Ford's walls before 1925, yet Henry refused to open his eyes. By the time he did it was too late.

The Model T's highly anticipated successor, the Model A, probably stood a good chance of stopping Chevrolet's charge had it only shown up a few years earlier than it did. Henry then did not help matters at all by completely closing down production in May 1927 to prepare for the A's epic introduction. Six months later the historic 1928 Model A was unveiled to a wide-eyed public on December 2.

At the same time Knudsen was presiding over the sale of more than a million Chevys for 1927. For the first time in its 15-year history Chevrolet soared to the industry's top sales spot, a place Ford had been familiar with for 20 years. Production-line problems at Ford allowed Chevrolet to top the charts with ease a second time in 1928 before the Model A got rolling and carried the former champ back into the limelight in 1929.

1923 Lincoln Model L

On February 4, 1922, Ford bought out Leland's Lincoln Motor Company, then wallowing in receivership, for $8 million. Just as Ford had fumed after Leland was brought in to "save" the Henry Ford Company in 1902, Leland too chafed under the younger Henry's influence in 1922. Leland left the reformed Lincoln venture after only four months, leaving Ford to put his son, Edsel, in control of his new luxury division.

Founded by Leland in 1920, Lincoln had represented a red-ink bath from the outset. A late start that year (production began in September) and a failure to meet initial production predictions did not inspire confidence among the firm's skittish board of directors. They then wasted little time hanging out a "For Sale" sign even before Leland had the chance to work the same engineering magic he had previously performed at Cadillac.

Although numbers did surge after the Ford buyout, the pairing of Detroit's cheapest, most simplistic and massively produced model line with one of its more finely engineered, pricier, limited-production offerings remained a shaky proposition, especially so after the Depression came along to further stain Lincoln's blotter in red. By 1930 Fords were making up 40 per cent of the market, while upscale Lincoln's share was a microscopic 0.17

per cent. Throughout the 1920s and 1930s Dearborn's rich coffers served as an ever-present crutch allowing Lincoln to lose as much as $4.6 million in 1931 and still stay rolling.

Back in 1922, only 150 Model L Lincolns rolled off the line in January and February, but 5,512 more followed during the rest of the year under Ford control. The cars Edsel Ford initially had control over then were basically Leland carryovers wearing new badges up front with the "Lincoln" name now squeezed between "Ford" and "Detroit."

The first "all-Ford" Model L Lincolns appeared in 1923 featuring only a few minor improvements, not a bad thing considering that the Leland engineering legacy continued running strong, as did his big 357 cubic-inch V8 with its "fork-and-blade" connecting rods. This innovative (and costly) design allowed cylinders to sit perfectly opposed from each other bank-to-bank. This layout helped make the Lincoln V8 one of Detroit's smoothest-running powerplants. Under Edsel Ford's direction Lincoln engineering continued to gain status, as did the car's image as one of America's finest luxury automobiles.

1925 Model T Runabout Pickup

SPECIFICATIONS

Engine: 20-horsepower 176.7 cubic-inch L-head four-cylinder

Bore & stroke: 3.75 x 4.00 inches

Compression: 3.98:1

Brakes: mechanical drums in rear only

Suspension: transverse buggy springs, front and rear, with heavier nine-leaf spring in place of the standard Model T in back

Price: $281

Wheelbase: 100 inches

Weight: 1,471 pounds

Model availability: two-door roadster half-ton pickup truck

Production: 33,759

Henry Ford basically ignored the truck market for 15 years; perhaps he was too busy building Model Ts as fast as Americans could grab them off the end of the assembly line. The first factory-built truck, Ford's Model TT one-ton, did not appear until 1917, by which time independent firms had sprung up to supply Model T owners with conversion kits to transform their Flivvers into light-duty utility vehicles or heavy-duty one-ton haulers. These aftermarket businesses continued to flourish into the 1920s because Ford's Model TT was sold only in bare-chassis form. Ford also continued to overlook customers interested in a light-duty half-ton pickup, leaving them no choice but to build their own or buy a conversion.

The pickup market itself did not get rolling until the 1930s as the vast majority of buyers before then demanded truly large, hard-working models. The credit for creating the good ol' half-ton pickup goes to Ford. Introduced in April 1925, the "Model T Runabout with Pick-Up Body" was not much more than a Model T roadster with a small cargo box mounted in place of the car's rear deck. Nonetheless, this combination is recognized as America's first true pickup, primarily because it was sold complete from the factory with a real steel cab and bed. Although a "factory-built" pickup from Dodge appeared the year before, it did not qualify for milestone status due to an antiquated wooden body.

Nicely priced and wonderfully practical, the Model T pickup was an instant success. By 1930 Chevrolet had followed with a factory-complete half-ton, and others joined the fraternity later in the decade. Pickup popularity truly exploded after World War II. Total truck sales were hovering around one million by 1960, then surpassed two million in 1971. Thirty years later, cars and trucks share almost equal billing, and it was Ford that started it all.

1926 Ford Tri-Motor airplane

Henry Ford hated flying even more than farming, because in his opinion it was far too dangerous—the flying, not the farming. But just as he changed the way Americans looked at the automobile, he also played a similarly historic role in the airplane's emergence as safe, practical transportation.

Ford's list of aviation milestones is every bit as impressive as his automotive record. He was the first to privately offer regularly scheduled airmail delivery, the first to offer air-freight service, and the

bought William's company in August 1925, roughly six months after he had opened his Ford Airport in Dearborn and four months after Ford Airlines had begun operating commercial flights between its home port and Chicago and Cleveland. Ford's ground-breaking airport incorporated America's first two concrete runways.

Ford Airlines' first planes were Stout-built 2-AT models, single-engine craft capable of carrying a pilot plus four to six passengers. The 3-AT followed in

first to build a paved airport runway. He was even the first to hire flight attendants, and he also was responsible for the initiation of America's first cross-country airline network. World War I then brought demand from overseas for U.S.-manufactured aircraft. Henry saw airborne craft as perhaps being a deterrent to conflict. He proposed a production run of a whopping 150,000 planes using his assembly line techniques, all aimed at preventing hostilities, not promoting them.

Henry never built those planes, nor did he wipe out war, but he did finally get into the aviation business after investing in the efforts of innovator William Stout in 1922. With support (both financial and otherwise) from Edsel Ford, Stout founded the Stout Metal Airplane Company in November that year to build all-metal airplanes.

Henry was impressed with Stout's work, so much so he finally

November 1925 in an attempt to increase capacity. Called a monstrosity by Henry Ford, this clumsy, stub-nosed, fat flyer featured three engines, and thus came the famous "Tri-Motor" name.

The 3-AT was an utter failure, but Ford's first successful Tri-Motor, the 4-AT-4, left the ground running in June 1926. Quickly nicknamed the "Tin Goose" due to its metal construction, the 4-AT-4 was America's first all-metal, multi-engined air transport.

Durable, strong and sure, Ford's Tri-Motor instantly became the mainstay of this country's burgeoning airline industry. These lumbering high-winged planes owned the skies up until the Boeing 247 took off in 1933—the last year for Henry's old airplane. Later airline pioneers were far more prolific (less than 200 Tri-Motors were built between 1926 and 1933), but the Tri-Motors place in aviation history remains secure for its role in opening up the skyways to everyday travelers.

1928 Model A Two-Door 'Tudor'

After leaving assembly plants idle since May 1927, Henry Ford finally introduced a replacement for the tired, old Tin Lizzie on December 2. Within 36 hours after it was officially announced in a $2 million advertising blitz, reportedly 10 million people rushed into showrooms to see for themselves. The leap in improvement from the Model T meant a rebirth for Ford, so Henry went back to the beginning of the alphabet, like his first car in 1903, the latest automobile out of Dearborn would be the "Model A."

The Model A's roots ran back to 1926 when it became obvious that the venerable Model T was no longer capable of staying ahead of its challenger from GM. But rewriting Detroit's greatest success story was not to be done overnight, unless, that is, you worked for Henry Ford. Although some development work predated May 1927, Ford shut the doors on his company after the last Model T was built and went to work, almost from scratch, constructing his Model A. The result was yet another automotive milestone.

Like the Model T, it was small and affordable, but that is where the likeness ended. Thanks to Edsel Ford's fashion-conscious influence, the Model A appealed to both the average buyer, and people such as New York governor Franklin Roosevelt and actress Mary Pickford.

Mechanical refinements were far too plentiful to be listed here. Highlights included a sturdier frame and a more powerful four-cylinder engine, and the A's four-wheel brakes, distributor ignition and three-speed sliding-gear transmission were company firsts. Two new bodystyles, the two-door "Tudor" and four-door "Fordor" sedans emerged as Ford's most popular offerings, proving that the fully-closed car's day had come. The more exciting, less convenient roadster very soon faded from the scene.

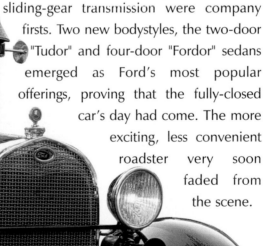

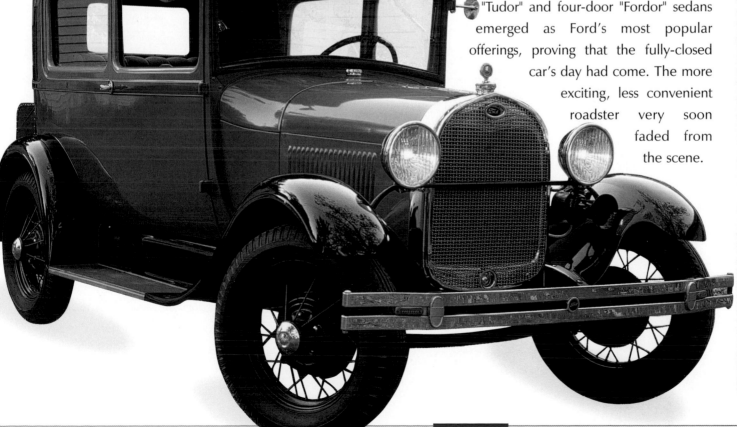

SPECIFICATIONS

Engine: 40-horsepower 200 cubic-inch L-head four-cylinder

Bore & stroke: 3.875 x 4.25 inches

Compression: 4.22:1

Fuel Delivery: Holley or Zenith two-barrel carburetor

Transmission: three-speed sliding-gear type with floor shifter

Suspension: transverse buggy springs and solid axles, front and rear

Brakes: mechanical four-wheel, foot pedal operated

Price: $585

Wheelbase: 103.5 inches

Weight: 2,386 pounds

Model availability: four-door, four-passenger sedan

Construction: body on frame

Production: 82,349 (in calendar year)

1931-40: Three's Company

"Like so many others, Edsel had recognized a need to replace the obsolete Model T well before its 1927 swan song. Yet his father would have nothing of it..."

ABOVE: *Henry Ford had been deeply reluctant to produce a multi-cylinder engine, but the instant popularity of Chevrolet's six persuaded him to go one better - two, in fact..*

ABOVE, RIGHT: *Model A production ceased in 1931 to make way for the all-new, V8 powered Model 18. The four cylinder engine was fitted in the same body and designated the Model B.*

Chevrolet's surge, the Great Depression and Henry Ford's increasingly obstinate refusal to leave the past behind all worked in concert to help transform the 1930s into tough times for the company that not all that long before had been building more cars than the rest of the industry combined. Ford people had been more or less unfamiliar with competitive pressures prior to 1925—to that point no other manufacturer even came within shouting distance of not just America's leading auto factory but the world's. Then they suddenly found themselves looking up to a rival two years later. Although the Model A did come along to turn things around in 1928, Ford's rise back to the top was short-lived. After leading the way in 1929 and 1930, Henry's firm was again passed by Chevrolet and would only see industry leadership (from a calendar-year sales perspective) once more during the decade, in 1935.

Plain and simple, the story would have been different had Henry just backed off and let his free-thinking chief officer run the show. But Edsel Ford's presidency had been a sham all along. The boss remained the boss regardless of title, and this boss rarely allowed someone else to dictate his decisions, even if that someone was his son.

Like so many others, Edsel had recognized a need to replace the obsolete Model T well before its 1927 swan song. Yet his father would have nothing of it until it was too late. Edsel also campaigned for a new car to fill the gap between low-priced Ford and high-line Lincoln, a vehicle that would compete with Studebaker and two newly born rivals, GM's Pontiac and Walter Chrysler's Dodge. Yet the old man again

put his foot down, and it was not until 1939 that the mid-priced Mercury finally debuted. Edsel and his engineers watched as competitors continually modernized their machines with cutting-edge features like hydraulic brakes, independent front suspensions and all-steel bodies. Yet Henry still stuck to his "less is more" ideal—simplicity had served his record-setting Model T so darned well for so darned long, why change anything now?

But Henry Ford could only hold back progress for so long. As much as he hated change, he finally did allow Edsel's styling team to begin annual model makeovers in 1933, in order to keep up with Detroit's styling leader, General Motors. GM's technically superior all-steel "turret-top" bodies appeared next in 1936; Ford designers then replaced that familiar fabric insert overhead with a roof made of solid steel the following year. And, lo and behold, modern hydraulic brakes did finally become standard Ford features in 1939.

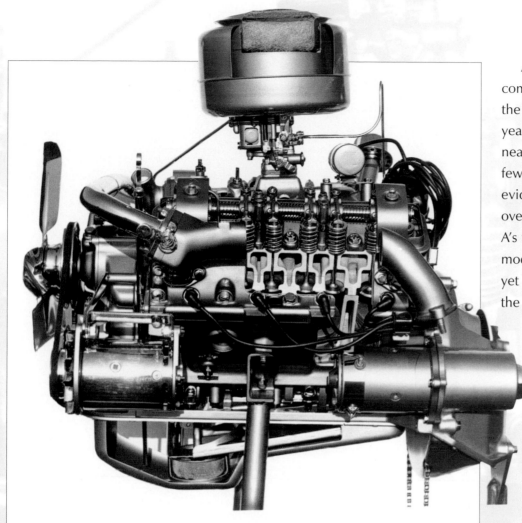

ABOVE: *Introduced in 1932 and produced entirely "in house" the Ford V8 displaced 221 cubic inches and developed 65 bhp @ 3400 rpm.*

All that aside, Henry's most notable concession to competitive pressures had come earlier in the decade, and the roots of this historic change actually ran back some 10 years before that. Like the Model T it powered along for nearly 20 years, Ford's good ol' four-cylinder engine ran a few years longer than it should have, a truth made especially evident after Chevrolet introduced its headline-making overhead-valve six-cylinder in 1929 to steal away the Model A's thunder. Costing only slightly more than the four-cylinder models it replaced, the new Chevy Six had everyone talking, yet Henry remained unimpressed. As he once growled during the T's heyday, "I've got no use for a motor that has more spark plugs than a cow has teats."

Maybe so, but his engineers had been directed to experiment with future power sources as early as 1921, and some of these relied on eight spark plugs. Apparently the boss had decided that if he did have to change, he would do so in a big way. Once word got out about Chevy's upcoming "Stovebolt," his position became firm: "We're going to go from a four to an eight, because Chevrolet is going to a six."

To double the cylinder count Ford demanded that his engineers do something that had never been done before: mass-produce an affordable monoblock V8. Cast-iron monoblock V8s had appeared earlier but at costs beyond Ford's scope and in numbers too small to matter due to casting complexities that limited production speeds. Most experts believed Henry's goal was unattainable; Charles Sorensen felt otherwise.

Ford's production chief, Sorensen had first gone to work for Henry in 1905, and he later played a major role in making the Model T's assembly line work. Within two decades, he had risen to one of the top two or three positions in the company, and by 1931 it had become his job to manufacture yet

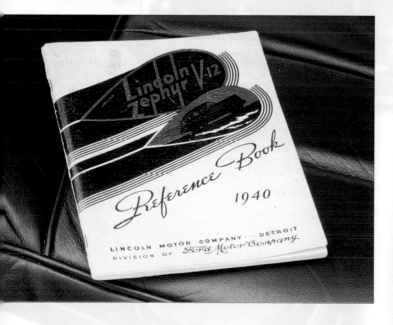

LEFT: *The Zephyr's 267.3 cubic inch flathead V12 was similar to the Ford V8 but with a narrower (75 degree) angle.*

ABOVE: *The Mercury, introduced in 1939 to fill the price gap between Ford and Lincoln, was billed as the car that dares to ask "Why?"*

ABOVE: *This end-of-the-line, 1931 Model A pick-up was hopefully employed in a dry-weather state...*

ABOVE: *The 1936 Lincoln Zephyr Sedan represented luxury and refinement at a bargain price: a V12 for $1,320.*

"The NRA included provisions that endorsed worker unionization. However, in 1935 the U.S. Supreme Court ruled that the NRA was unconstitutional."

another milestone, America's first low-priced V8.

In short order Sorensen perfected an all-new complicated-yet-quick casting process that both made the cheap V8 possible and earned him the nickname "Cast-Iron Charlie." "It was a revolutionary method, developed entirely within the Ford organization," he later said. "There was nothing like it anywhere else on a comparable scale."

Henry Ford reportedly spent $50 million to upgrade the River Rouge foundry in preparation for V8 mass production, and it was money well spent. Once up and running, the Rouge casting facility was spitting out 3,000 V8 cylinder blocks a day, a phenomenal number.

Big numbers remained a trademark at Ford into the 1930s, though not all were positive. Henry's 20 millionth car was built in 1931 and 5 million Model A's were on the road by 1932. On the other side of the coin, corporate losses that year amounted to $75 million. A Depression-riddled economy made 1932 an awful year for automakers, but Henry made matters worse by shutting down his plants (this time for nearly four months) in preparation for the V8, which debuted in March.

Despite rave reviews, Ford's historic engine was inhibited by teething problems that allowed the Chevy Six to hold the industry lead. Henry had sold "only" one million V8s by 1934—a definite disappointment in Ford terms, but a fabulous score from the perspective of most other automakers, many of which would not survive the decade. Ford, however, went back into the black in 1934 and then jumped in front of Chevrolet the following year.

Reportedly the company lost $120 million from 1931 to 1933, but perhaps even more damaging was a loss of public trust. Like so many other industrialists of the day, Henry Ford became well acquainted with labor strife during the 1930s, this after he had been lauded as the working man's hero a decade or so before.

Declining demand in certain regions first became apparent in 1930, a year that Ford claimed more than 40 per cent of industry sales, even as its annual production was falling off by nearly 25 per cent. The fall then turned into a dive as 1931 production did not reach half of 1930's total. Desperate times brought desperate measure, and on July 29, 1931, Henry was forced to lay off 75,000 workers and close down 25 of

his 36 U.S. plants. That was shortly followed by wage cutbacks in October for the remaining employees, all of whom found themselves out of work after all the facilities shut down to prepare for the V8's introduction.

Though many went back to work in March 1932, a good number remained unemployed after the V8 went into production, and between 3,000 and 5,000 of these people chose to publicize their plight by embarking on a "hunger march" on March 7. The workers who showed up at River Rouge's Gate #3 were met by the police and Ford's new "Service Department" security force, trouble broke out during the protest and four protestors died during the violence, and more than 50 people were injured. Among the latter was Henry's righthand man, Harry Bennett, who headed the Service Department. Bennett survived the incident to clash again with workers five years later.

ABOVE: *This 1932 Ford V8 Flathead looks sedate in this tranquil setting, but it was a hot-rodder's dream.*

Meanwhile, bad news continued coming from Henry Ford's office. More production cutbacks were announced in November 1932, and within two months only six of the 30 plants that had been in operation that summer were open for business.

Things then grew worse, at least from Henry's perspective, after Congress passed the National Industrial Recovery Act in June 1933. One of Franklin Roosevelt's many "New Deal" strategies, the NRA included provisions that endorsed worker unionization. However, in 1935 the U.S. Supreme Court ruled that the NRA was unconstitutional, but Ford could not stop union inroads into his workforce.

On May 26, 1937, United Auto Workers organizers distributing handbills to Ford employees clashed with Harry Bennett's Service Department, an event that served to further stain Henry Ford's once revered image, as well as galvanize his workforce in favor of unionization. That battle, however, had already lost front-page space to a far greater conflict then going on halfway around the world.

ABOVE AND RIGHT: *Ford continued to offer choice and versatility in the new V8 range as it had in the days of the Model T. This V8 pick-up dates from 1939.*

1932-34 Lincoln KB

As frivolously small as Lincoln might have appeared early on in the giant shadow of its parent company, Ford's "little" luxury line did have an awful lot going for itself as it entered the 1930s. First and foremost was Henry Leland's legacy, a renown reputation for precision engineering and high-class construction demonstrated most prominently in durable, dignified fashion by the car's smooth, strong, silent-running V8. Second was Edsel Ford's undying devotion to keeping Leland's dreams alive and making his own come true in high style; unlike his mechanically minded father, Edsel was a man of sophisticated tastes and a keen eye for classic lines and timeless design.

Introduced in response to Cadillac's stunning new V16 Cadillac of 1930, the nicely modernized, much more grand Model K replaced Lincoln's old, somewhat stoic Model L. Though it still relied on basically the same V8 created by Leland some 10 years earlier, the new K's long, low, more graceful body rode on a truly royal wheelbase stretched to 145 inches, nine more than the Model L's hub-to-hub measurement. At 385 cubic inches, engine displacement carried over from the L to the K, but output went up from 90 to 120 horsepower thanks to a compression boost and the installation of a dual-downdraft carburetor, a first for the industry.

The tried-and-tested Lincoln V8 was boosted further to 125 horsepower for the first Model KA, introduced in 1932. Edsel Ford's design team cut costs by using the old Model L's shorter 136-inch wheelbase as a foundation. Less proved to be more as the relatively affordable KA "buoyed" Lincoln sales in 1932, the year the entire automotive industry bottomed out at its worst. While sales at Packard and Cadillac were dropping by 32 and 44 per cent, respectively, Lincoln's decline for 1932 was a marginal 9 per cent.

The classic KB also came along in 1932 as a flagship intended to prove that Ford's luxury division was no impostor, and belonged right up alongside Cadillac. To that end, Lincoln's chief engineer Frank Johnson, working in concert with Fred Wellborn and Jack Wharam,

created a new engine for the KB, a powerful V12 that nearly matched Cadillac's best and biggest in size—448 cubic inches compared to 453—even with four less cylinders. Output was 150 horsepower, 15

less than the V16 from Cadillac yet more than enough brute force to move nearly three tons of luxury motorcar to nearly 100 mph, a major accomplishment for the day.

Former Brewster body man Henry Crecelius was in charge of dressing up the Lincoln V12. Factory-supplied bodies were available, but the best came from independent coachbuilders, who were also experiencing their zenith at the time before quickly disappearing from the American automotive scene before World War II. Famous firms like Brunn, Judkins, Willoughby, Waterhouse, Deitrich and LeBaron supplied everything from two-door convertible roadsters to palatial four-door limousines.

Standard Lincoln-supplied touches for all 1932 KB models included an attractive rounded radiator shell, parking lamps mounted on each front fender, and "doors" in the hoodside panels instead of louvers. When the KB returned for 1933 it featured an even better-looking rakish radiator shell and a return to louvered hoods. Additional adornment included hidden horns, "freestanding" (no tiebar) headlights, and stylish "skirts" for the front fenders. Meant to hide the frame, those fad-conscious skirts first appeared in February 1933, but could have been added by dealers to KB Lincolns built prior to that month. Beneath the 1933 KB went a redesigned X-member frame that relied on an equally trendy "double-drop" design to help make the KB appear even lower and sleek.

Even though the second-edition Model KB represented an improvement over the first, Lincoln still could not sell such an expensive automobile in such hard times. A production total of 1,515 in 1932 could have been considered healthy considering the circumstances. At only 613, 1933's total was disappointing to say the least. KB sales improved to 754 in 1934, then Lincoln dropped the official KB/KA designations the next year. All Lincoln Ks used a V12 beginning in 1934. Sales dwindled rapidly after 1936, the last was delivered in 1940.

Lincoln's early KB models are still revered as probably the finest automobiles ever created under the direction of the man who knew a little about fine things, Edsel Ford. And at the price, they may have also represented the best of the best from a decade that featured its fair share of very fine cars, immortal classics all.

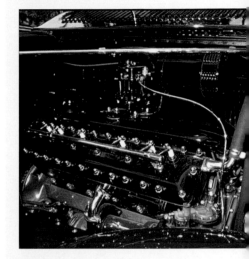

1935 Ford Cabriolet

Henry Ford's original ideal involved simplicity, and it did not get much simpler than the Model T, but what worked so well in the T's heyday did not stand up at all by the time the 1920s were winding down. The emergence of Chevrolet and the Great Depression reformed the way business was done in Dearborn. Selling cars in the 1930s was no longer so simple, and staying at the top required something Henry never liked: continual change.

While nothing from Ford before World War II would make bigger headlines than the "flathead" V8's introduction in 1932, various rapid-fire upgrades were made seemingly every year to keep pace with Chevrolet. Yet another new chassis and body showed up in 1933, along with a much improved flathead.

Henry's restyled, revamped 1935 Model 48 was introduced on December 27, 1934, at the New York Auto Show. Far and away the most stylish Dearborn product yet, it was the result of Edsel Ford's growing presence. He had been overseeing Ford styling since the Model A's development, which evolved at a time when Dearborn officially did not even have a styling group. Veteran engineer Joe Galamb, the man behind the Model T, did the bulk of the Model A styling work, under Edsel's close direction.

Then in 1932, Edsel hired Eugene T. "Bob" Gregorie, a young draftsman who became one of Detroit's styling immortals. In 1935, Gregorie became head of Ford's first in-house design department, formed by Edsel two years before in response to GM's trend-setting Art & Colour Section, set up in 1927 and headed by the legendary Harley Earl. Gregorie's team originally included three members or so but was employing as many as 20 stylists by 1938. Though GM would be recognized as Detroit's styling leader for many decades to come, Ford was certainly no slouch after Gregorie's rise to prominence.

The famously freshened 1935 Fords, not only looked fabulous, they also impressed buyers more than ever, even though much of the platform remained familiar. Mechanical brakes, a solid beam axle up front, and Henry's traditional transverse "buggy" springs at both ends continued on. All told, the 1935 package represented what the ad guys called "Greater Beauty, Greater Comfort, and Greater Safety." Dearborn production nearly doubled that year as Chevrolet drivers went back to watching the southern ends of a whole lot of northbound Fords.

1939 Mercury

Advertisements called it "the car that dares to ask 'Why?'" Perhaps the better question was "why not sooner?" Why had not Ford introduced the Mercury line before 1939? Detroit's lower-medium price class had been running strong for nearly 10 years by then, yet there was not one model in this growing field. Both Edsel Ford, and Jack Davis, Ford's sales manager, had long been aware of the major gap in their company's model lines, a hole that remained wide open after the Lincoln-Zephyr V-12 appeared in 1936. Like Davis, Edsel knew the logical "stopgap" was an upscale Ford, not a lesser Lincoln.

Work finally began in relative earnest on what would become the Mercury in the summer of 1937. Legend has it that many, many labels were considered for this new car before Edsel finally named it after the "winged messenger" from Roman mythology. Edsel's initial choice was "Ford-Mercury," in keeping with his Lincoln-Zephyr approach, but the name became simply "Mercury" by the time it was introduced to the press in October 1938.

Though press critics initially claimed the 1939 Mercury looked "like a half-sister

to the Lincoln Zephyr," the new model line was in truth more closely related to its low-priced cousin. Its stretched wheelbase was four inches longer than Ford's, compared to a noticeable nine inches shorter than Lincoln-Zephyr's. Pricing was about $160 more than a Ford, and about $430 less than a Lincoln-Zephyr. For that extra cash, a Mercury buyer got an attractive automobile that was slightly longer, wider and heavier than a Ford. Yet it remained every bit as strong and relatively fuel-efficient as its entry-level brethren.

Like all new Fords in 1939, the first Mercury also came standard with Lockheed hydraulic brakes. As for those obsolete "buggy springs," solid beam axle in front and torque-tube drive, both the new Mercury and existing Ford lines would have to wait until after Henry's death to cut their last ties to the dusty past.

SPECIFICATIONS

Engine: 95-horsepower 239 cubic-inch L-head V8

Bore and stroke: 3.19 x 3.75 inches

Compression: 6.15:1

Fuel delivery: single downdraft two-barrel carburetor

Transmission: three-speed sliding-gear with floor shifter

Price: $916 to $1,018

Wheelbase: 116 inches

Weight: 2,995 to 3,013 pounds

Model availability: two-door convertible, coupe and sedan; four-door sedan

Construction: all-steel body on double-drop X-member frame

Production: 69,135 all models

1940 Lincoln Continental Cabriolet

Edsel Ford returned from a European trek in September 1938 with an image stuck in his head of yet another unique automobile built personally for him. This time, inspiration came from various styling trends he had noticed overseas. As stylist E.T. "Bob" Gregorie later remembered, the cabriolet his boss wanted built had to be "strictly continental." In Gregorie's words, the automobile also had to be a "dignified car," yet one that looked "fast and active, sporting, exhilarating." More importantly, it simply had to be completed in time for Edsel and Eleanor's next vacation to Florida in March 1939, giving Gregorie and crew only six months to do the trick.

Gregorie suggested the base for Edsel's cabriolet should be the Lincoln-Zephyr, already revered for its ground-breaking styling. From there, Gregorie added and subtracted to achieve the look Edsel envisioned. Off went the running boards, on went a squared-off trunk that loaded from the top.

Away went a three-inch section of the body at the beltline to dramatically lower the car's overall height. In went seven inches to the hood's length, making the already low machine appear even lower. The finishing touch came in the form of an exposed spare tire on the back, a truly "continental" feature Edsel insisted on.

Completed in February 1939, Edsel's latest dream machine was delivered south to the vacationing couple. Legend has it that friends and neighbors all wanted one of these lovely cabriolets for their very own, convincing Edsel to order limited production of his one-off custom-

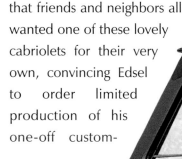

bodied Lincoln-Zephyr. Less romantic types insist he had always probably planned his cabriolet as a pre-production prototype. Either way, the decision was made in April 1939 to produce the "Lincoln-Zephyr Continental" in limited quantities as a 1940 model.

Two pre-production Continental cabriolets—by then based on the restyled 1940 Lincoln-Zephyr—were built in September 1939, and completed in time for public introductions at the Ford Rotunda in Dearborn on October 3 and at the New York and Los Angeles auto shows two weeks later. The first regular-production Continental, intended for actor Jackie Cooper, left the line on December 13. Apparently only 25 Continental carbiolets were built during those last few months of 1939. Then a coupe joined the cabriolet in May 1940. Total production for the 1940 Continental was 350 cabriolets, 54 coupes.

The Continental returned—with the Zephyr reference gone—in 1941. A restyled body emerged in 1942 just before World War II abruptly ended production on February 2. Looking much like the 1942 model, the 1946 model emerged after the end of the war and carried on in similar fashion until it was discontinued after 1948. Plans for keeping the Continental legacy alive beyond that point were made but never fulfilled.

SPECIFICATIONS

Engine: *292 cubic-inch L-head V-12*

Transmission: *three-speed manual*

Price: *$2,916*

Wheelbase: *125 inches*

Height: *62 inches*

Weight: *3,860 pounds.*

Model availability: *two-door cabriolet*

Production: *350*

1941-50: War and Peace

"Defense contract dollars revitalized America's auto industry almost overnight after 10 years of slow recovery following the Wall Street crash of 1929. Ford was soon turning out the weapons of war at unheard-of rates, and the technical lessons learned on those rapid-fire production lines promised great things to come."

He may have hated war, but Henry Ford apparently did not mind conflict in his own world. His career was seemingly one historic confrontation after another: with Henry Leland, with Alexander Malcomson, with the Selden patent group, with James Couzens, with the Dodge brothers, with William Knudsen, with disgruntled out-of-work employees, with F.D.R.'s policies (both foreign and domestic); with UAW organizers—and with his son, Edsel.

For many years Henry certainly did know what was best for Ford, and millions upon millions of Model Ts were rolling proof. But as times changed, the main man did not. On top of that Henry was not getting any younger, he turned 75 in July 1938 and suffered a stroke the same year. By 1940 it was clear to many that Henry's influence was doing much more harm than good to the stumbling corporate giant that had once stood head and shoulders above the rest.

Yet he refused to loosen his grip, to let his talented people do what they did best. Edsel had so much to offer, to both his father and his father's company, but the old man fought him tooth and nail every chance he got. And to add injury to insult, Henry sought out support from his henchman, Harry Bennett, instead of his own blood when things started getting tough in the early 1930s. Bennett's rise to power signaled a truly bizarre twist to the tale, and who knows to what depths his strong-arm tactics would have taken the company had not the Pearl Harbor attack dragged America into World War II in December 1941.

Defense contract dollars then revitalized America's auto industry almost overnight after 10 years of slow recovery following the Wall Street crash of November 1929. Like its rivals in Detroit, Ford Motor Company was soon turning out the weapons of war at unheard-of rates, and the technical lessons learned on those rapid-fire production lines promised great things to come once peace returned. In Ford's case, however, modernized plants and processes could not possibly compensate for its top-office turmoil, which took another turn for the worse after 50-year-old Edsel Ford died of stomach cancer in May 1943.

Five days later, on June 1, Edsel's grieving father, soon to turn 80, was re-elected to company president, a seat he had given up to his son nearly 25 years before. Of course Henry had remained in charge all along, but with Edsel gone, there now was no buffer between the elder

ABOVE: *Henry Ford was deeply reluctant to move to war production until after Japan's pre-emptive strike against Pearl Harbor.*

Ford's fading faculties and the stark realities of a rapidly changing world. Beyond that, it was the black-hatted Bennett who actually gained control, and this particular reality frightened both the entire Ford family and a federal government that was counting on the corporation for its massive support of the war effort.

Enter Edsel's oldest son, Henry Ford II, then serving in the U.S. Navy. Fearing the failure of one of America's largest employers, Washington officials secured an early discharge for Ford's 25-year-old grandson in July 1943 and brought him back home to right the sinking ship. Henry, however, would have nothing of it, nor, of course, would Bennett, who had his own intentions of replacing Ford senior. Henry II's initial position was a token one and remained so until 1944.

It was then left to Henry II's grandmother, Clara Ford, to intervene, something she was no stranger to. In June 1941 Clara had threatened to leave her husband of 53 years if he did not sign the unionization agreement that he had battled against throughout the 1930s. A wildcat strike had shut down River Rouge in April, action that had convinced Edsel Ford that it was finally time put the issue to a vote. He had managed to convinced his father of the same, after which 97 per cent

ABOVE: *Ford's immediate post-war advertising encouraged Americans to look forward to a brighter tomorrow.*

LEFT AND ABOVE RIGHT: *The radical, 1949 restyle can be credited in large part to "freelance" influence. Those employed included George Walker, working alongside the legendary Elwood Engel but it was Richard Caleal's design that won the day.*

BELOW: *The "waterfall" radiator went wide-screen in 1942. Running boards finally disappeared. The Super DeLuxe had its radiator accented by color-coded inserts.*

of the workforce said yes to UAW membership. Nonetheless, old Henry could not bring himself to sign off on the deal, but then Clara delivered on her ultimatum. "Don't ever discredit the power of a woman," said Mr. Ford after he inked the agreement on June 20, making it the automobile industry's first closed-shop union contract.

Clara's power again came into play after Henry II's return from the Navy. She insisted that her husband resign and allow new blood to take over, but he did not respond until Edsel's widow, Eleanor Clay, joined forces with her mother-in-law in favor of the changeover. Eleanor threatened that her one-third share of Ford Motor Company would go up for sale if her son was not allowed more control. Henry again capitulated; Henry II was appointed executive vice president in January 1944 and then became president in September 1945. Among his first acts was to see Harry Bennett to the door, after he had weeded out all his supporters from the company.

Unfortunately other more important figures had also made their way out that same doorway by then. Among these were engineer Laurence Sheldrick and Edsel's styling chief, Bob Gregorie, both in September 1943. Charles Sorenson, himself with ambitions to take Henry Ford's place, left in March 1944. When peace did come in August 1945, Henry II found himself in charge of a car company in an even worse mess than it had been in before the war.

Fortunately enough for Ford Americans then were starving for new cars. No one cared that all 1946 automobiles rolling out of Detroit were just made-over pre-war

After absorbing losses of $8.1 million in 1946, Ford raked in $64.8 million in profits the following year at the height of a postwar seller's market."

RIGHT: *The "Woody" remained popular right through the 1950s. This is a 1949 Custom, two-door station wagon.*

ABOVE: *The bonus for Ford's truck division in 1948 was the U.S.'s massive construction program.*

ABOVE: *Express Delivery, courtesy of the elegant, 1953 Crestline van.*

ABOVE: *The 1942 DeLuxe station wagon was a substantial and practical piece of equipment.*

models. And in Ford's case that meant the same antiquated features Henry had refused to update, prior to Pearl Harbor, were back for an encore. No problem, at least at first. After absorbing losses of $8.1 million in 1946, Ford raked in $64.8 million in profits the following year at the height of a postwar seller's market.

But even a blind man could see that buyers would not take leftovers for long. Indeed, 1948 was a terrible year for Ford Motor Company as Chrysler for the first time managed to slip past into the second spot in sales behind General Motors. Blaming Ford's tired, old products was not entirely fair, though, as Henry II cut short the 1948 model year to hasten the arrival of a new era for all three of his model lines, a historic rebirth that his grandfather did not live to see.

Henry Ford died in April 1947. His wife Clara followed him three years later. With Henry finally at peace, there was nothing left behind but new blood. And new ideas. Henry Ford II had wasted little time surrounding himself with new people after rising to power in 1945. It was this group's youth and enthusiasm that earned them the nickname "Whiz Kids." Included were Charles "Tex" Thornton, Gene Anderson, George Moore, Robert McNamara, Ben Davis Mills, Arjay Miller, James Wright, and Francis Reith, to name a few. Though unknown to the industry in 1946, many of the Whiz Kids soon made big names for themselves: McNamara and Miller later served as Ford presidents, Wright went on to become Ford Division general manager, Reith ran Mercury, and Mills did the same at Lincoln.

Henry II also looked to rival companies for experience. First came Ernest Breech, who left GM's Bendix division to become Ford's executive vice president in July 1946. Breech was quickly followed by other GM defectors, including Oldsmobile engineer Harold Youngren, Chevrolet stylist Eugene Bordinat, designer George Snyder (also from Olds), and Lewis Crusoe, formerly GMs' assistant treasurer. With all the right people in place, it then became a matter of committing the tens of millions of dollars needed to retool the entire line-up, which Henry II's new team of designers and engineers did in nearly record time.

The first all-new postwar Lincolns and Mercurys went on sale in April 1948, followed by the sensational all-new Fords in June. Though GM had beaten Ford out of the blocks with its new postwar cars, the boys from Dearborn encountered little difficulty drawing raves for their redesigned 1949 models. Some teething problems typically showed up, but they were quickly ironed out as Ford accountants were kept busy totaling up the year's profits at $177 million. Then in 1950, Dearborn officials laid claim to a healthy 24 per cent market share, easily the highest since the mid-1930s. So it turns out that the Ford women knew best: the future was safe in Henry II's hands.

1943 Army Jeep

Separated from the grim reality by two oceans, most U.S. citizens could only imagine the nightmare that was World War II. Instead of facing the horrors firsthand, Americans fought the battle by helping build the greatest war machine ever seen.

In Dearborn, memories of "Tin Lizzies" rolling off an assembly line en masse were swept away by what was happening at Ford's enormous Willow Run plant, where Consolidated B-24 bombers were lumbering almost one an hour out the door by March 1944. Along with B-24s, Ford also mass-produced various military vehicles ranging from amphibious personnel carriers to light tanks. Most memorable among these machines was a lightweight, four-wheel-drive beast originally created by the American Bantam Car Company in Butler, Pennsylvania.

Even though Bantam initiated developmental work in 1940, it was Willys-Overland and Ford that ended up with the contracts to produce the real thing in large numbers for the Army—W-O built "MB" model Jeeps, while Ford's were labeled "GPW." Not only did the small Pennsylvania firm not get the deal, it did not even receive credit for creating the Jeep thanks to various unscrupulous Willys advertisements that claimed that honor.

Meanwhile, Dearborn's involvement in the whole process was being investigated even as its first GPW was being driven off the line by Edsel Ford on February 28, 1941. Many witnesses felt that, even though Henry Ford was disgusted by war morally and originally believed hostilities in Europe were just a ruse to allow Franklin Roosevelt control of his company, the old man would do anything to obtain such a promising defense contract, one that offered ample peacetime possibilities. As I.F. Stone claimed in *Nation* magazine, "behind Ford's eagerness to get the contract is the hope that after the war this midget car can be developed into an all-purpose farm machine which can pull a plow by day and take the family to the movies at night."

In the best interests of guaranteeing a strong demand for that "midget car" after the war, Ford reportedly even demanded that none of the Jeeps delivered for military duty overseas find their way back to American soil once peace broke out. As legend has it, countless Ford GPWs "accidentally" rolled off U.S.-bound ships into

the Pacific after Japan's surrender. In all, Ford was responsible for some 281,000 of the approximately 650,000 Jeeps built between 1941 and 1945. Mechanically the MB and GPW Jeeps were identical right down to their 54-horsepower Willys L-head four-cylinder engines. Ford's GPW could have been identified by its stamped steel one-piece grille and open "hat channel" frame member behind that grille. Willys MBs had slat grilles and used a tubular frame member. An even closer look also would have revealed various script "F" stampings and castings found throughout the GPW. It seems Henry Ford was especially concerned about what might happen should his Jeeps find their way into Allied hands, especially those pesky copycats from Moscow, and protecting patents was the goal.

Ford's contract to build GPWs expired on July 31, 1945, leaving Willys-Overland sole possession of the postwar market for civilian Jeeps. Later Kaiser, then American Motors, then Chrysler took it from there.

SPECIFICATIONS

Engine: Cast iron - 4 Cylinders in line

Displacement: 134.02 cubic inches

Bore and stroke: 3.13 x 4.38

Horsepower: 60

Body Styles: Convertible

No. of seats: 4+

Weight (lbs): "quarter ton"

Price: Government issue

Production: Willys 358,489 by 1945, Ford 277,896

1948 Ford F1 Pickup Truck

Fifty years are not 100, but they still represent a long time, especially so for a model-line legacy in Detroit. Even the best vehicles do not stick around nearly that long, not like Ford's F-series pickup truck. Dearborn's light truck line marked its 50th anniversary in 1998, and man was that some party. Festivities actually began in October 1997 when officials threw a wing-ding for the press during the State Fair of Texas in Dallas.

"I can think of no better place to celebrate the 50th birthday of America's favorite truck than right here in Texas, the heart of truck country," said Ford Division general manager Ross Roberts. Indeed the Lone Star State stands as the world's largest light truck market—more than 10 per cent of all full-sized pickups sold annually hit the road in Texas.

Texans always do seem to do things in a bigger way, and so it was only right to throw a really big party. A huge 50-foot-tall, three-layer mock birthday cake was served up at the State Fair in 1997, and concealed in its second layer was Ford's new 1998 F-150, the latest in a long line of America's best-selling vehicles, car or truck. By then the F-series pickup was also recognized as the world's best-selling nameplate of all time after having roared past the VW Beetle in 1995. More than 26 million F-series trucks had been sold by 1997, some worked to death by their owners, others treated to a kinder, gentler existence.

"Today's F-series competes in a marketplace that has changed considerably since the nameplate's introduction in 1948," said Ford strategic market analysis manager Joel Pitcoff in 1998. "No longer strictly a workhorse, the present F-series has taken its place as a family member and a pleasure companion."

Changed considerably? Today's pickups have replaced cars completely in many garages. In 1948 they were mostly found on farm lots and construction sites, but the competition to build the best trucks was every bit as tough then as it is now.

Chevrolet had beaten its Big Three rivals out of the blocks with America's first all-new postwar pickup in 1947. Ford's response then appeared the following year wearing all-new F-series labels that varied by load capacity. The half-ton was an "F-1," the one-ton was an "F-2," and so ending up at "F-8" for the big three-tonners.

A long list of improvements for Ford's new "Bonus Built" trucks included the "Million Dollar Cab," named after the investment Dearborn designers made while making the F-1

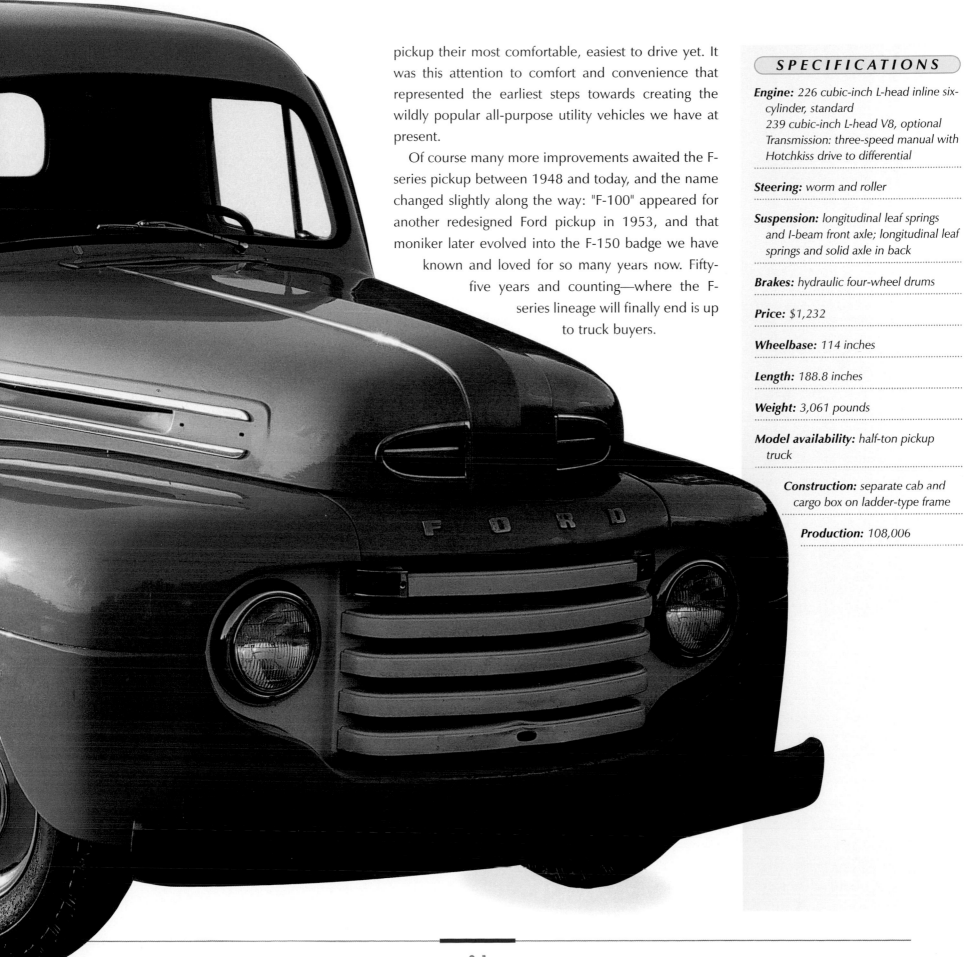

pickup their most comfortable, easiest to drive yet. It was this attention to comfort and convenience that represented the earliest steps towards creating the wildly popular all-purpose utility vehicles we have at present.

Of course many more improvements awaited the F-series pickup between 1948 and today, and the name changed slightly along the way: "F-100" appeared for another redesigned Ford pickup in 1953, and that moniker later evolved into the F-150 badge we have known and loved for so many years now. Fifty-five years and counting—where the F-series lineage will finally end is up to truck buyers.

SPECIFICATIONS

Engine: *226 cubic-inch L-head inline six-cylinder, standard*
239 cubic-inch L-head V8, optional
Transmission: *three-speed manual with Hotchkiss drive to differential*

Steering: *worm and roller*

Suspension: *longitudinal leaf springs and I-beam front axle; longitudinal leaf springs and solid axle in back*

Brakes: *hydraulic four-wheel drums*

Price: *$1,232*

Wheelbase: *114 inches*

Length: *188.8 inches*

Weight: *3,061 pounds*

Model availability: *half-ton pickup truck*

Construction: *separate cab and cargo box on ladder-type frame*

Production: *108,006*

1949 Lincoln

On April 22, 1948, Ford Motor Company kicked off the 1949 model year with the introduction of two all-new Lincolns; the short-wheelbase "junior" and the longer, more regal Cosmopolitan. Of the many changes the most notable were a completely revamped slabside body, a return to body-on-frame construction, and Lincoln's first V8 in 16 years.

Lincoln planners had got a big jump on 1949 new car production by secretly developing the future when they were supposed to be making war. In 1942, the Ford Family of Fine Cars crew, led by stylist E.T. Gregorie and engineer Laurence Sheldrick, went underground—so far underground not even Henry Ford knew what was going on. He threw a fit when he found out, he slapped Gregorie's wrists and had Sheldrick fired—not because they were operating contrary to the war effort but because their plans contradicted his ideal for the company's new postwar cars. While Henry was reportedly considering plans to do away with Lincoln and Mercury and market only an ultra-practical Ford model, the rest of the Ford family was pressing him to transfer control into more capable hands. By September 1945 Henry Ford II was president and Ernest Breech was executive vice president by 1946.

Breech needed only one look at Gregories' proposed postwar models to sense disaster— GMs' new models would leave the large, bulky Fords, Lincolns and Mercurys in the dust. But with production plans being far too advanced to make major changes, Breech proposed a downsizing of the new model line. The Continental was dropped from postwar plans, leaving the 125-inch wheelbase Cosmopolitan as the topline Lincoln. Next, the proposed 121-inch Mercury became the standard Lincoln, a car destined to do battle with the typical "mass market" luxury cars from Chrysler, Buick and Oldsmobile. The Mercury then dropped down onto the 118-inch chassis originally planned for the new 1949 Ford, leaving Dearborn's price leader without a frame. Breech's answer was a smaller 114-inch wheelbase.

Although both lines carried the same basic look, differences were many since the big Cosmopolitans were all Lincoln, while the junior versions were half Mercury. Cosmos got huge, curved one-piece windshields; juniors got typical two-piece flat glass. Cosmos got the heavy-duty, luxo-cruiser chassis; juniors got Mercury's less formidable foundation. Cosmos got super smooth, flowing slabside lines; juniors again got a taste of Mercury with a few extra crimps and trim pieces thrown in. As for similarities, both had a multitude of chassis improvements including independent front coil

spring suspension, longitudinal rear leaf springs, parallelogram-link steering, better brakes and a semi-floating Hotchkiss-drive rear axle with an open driveshaft. Both also got the "new" Lincoln V8.

At a time when GM was turning to lightweight, short-stroke overhead-valve V8s, Lincoln's L-head powerplant hardly represented "newness." Based on the 1948 337-cid Ford truck engine, the 1949 Lincoln

V8 was 200 pounds heavier than the 1949 Cadillac V8. Nonetheless, the L-head V8 did represent an improvement on the antiquated V12 it replaced. On the downside, Lincoln's new V8 was an infamous oil-burner, and early models fell victim to gremlins: poor fit and finish of the body led to various bangs and rattles, not to mention leaks around windows, doors and the trunk.

All that aside, the 1949 Lincolns sold like no Lincoln before, and like no Lincoln would for another 23 years. Along with 35,123 Cosmopolitans, the newly formed Lincoln-Mercury division sold 38,384 junior Lincolns for 1949—an amazing total for an automaker once dedicated to painstaking production of highly upscale, exclusive automobiles. Clearly a new era had begun.

SPECIFICATIONS

Engine: 152-horsepower 337 cubic-inch L-head V8

Bore & stroke: 3.5 x 4.37 inches

Fuel delivery: Holley two-barrel carburetor

Transmission: three-speed manual standard; GM-supplied Hydra-Matic automatic optional late in the year

Price: $3,116

Wheelbase: 121 inches

Weight: 4,224 pounds

Model availability: 1949 "Junior" Lincoln was offered as a two-door club coupe, four-door sport sedan and two-door convertible

Production: total for all three 1949 models was 38,384

1949 Ford

It was independent Studebaker down in South Bend, Indiana, that beat Detroit to the punch in 1947, becoming "first by far with a postwar car." Cadillac was the quickest in Big Three ranks to counter the all-new Stude, rolling out its equally new 1948 models in March that year. Ford's first postwar car, designated a 1949 model, finally showed up June, to the delight of both family members and customers alike. Young Henry Ford II had fortunately got a handle on things six years after being thrust into the mess created by his grandfather, and the all-new 1949 Lincolns, Mercurys and Fords were rolling proof.

Credit for the truly fresh 1949 Ford went to design and styling teams headed by engineering vice president Harold Youngren and outsider George Walker. Youngren's group produced a thoroughly modern chassis that finally left old

replaced by a lighter ladder-type frame with boxed side rails. Engine technology changed little, but brakes were markedly improved. On top of it all went a body that fully reflected Detroit's new taste for slab-sided styling. Uncluttered super-sleek lines were certainly new, as were longer, lower impressions, all of which helped the 1949 Ford garner the Fashion Academy Award that year.

American car-buyers, tired of all the pre-war leftovers that were sold from 1946 to 1948, loved the look. In 1949 1.1 million Fords rolled off showroom floors during an extended production run, helping the guys from Dearborn beat out their Bow-Tie-wearing rivals in model-year sales figures for the first time since 1937. But industry-leading popularity aside, the 1949 Ford did need some fixing. The all-new 1949s were rolled out in such haste, little time was afforded to ironing out the bugs. Various rattles, shakes, leaks and mechanical nuisances had to be addressed over the year. To their delight, the ironing was basically complete by 1950, with a few new folds thrown in for good measure.

Henry's transverse buggy springs, solid front axle, and torque tube behind. New updates included Hotchkiss drive, parallel A-arms with coil springs up front, and longitudinal leaf springs in back. While the familiar 114-inch wheelbase carried over from 1948, the old X-member foundation used prior to 1949 was

1949 Mercury

Mercury's first all-new postwar models debuted one week after running mate Lincoln's debut on April 29, 1948. Unlike earlier Mercurys, which shared sheetmetal with the lower line Fords, the 1949 cars showed off distinct family ties with the new, upscale Lincoln. Or at least the upscale "baby" Lincoln, not the top-shelf Cosmopolitan. Though the wheelbase varied by three inches between the junior Lincoln and the upgraded Mercury, most of the bodywork was the same. Different grilles and headlights set the two apart, the latter in a big way as the Lincoln used those radical recessed units.

All the modern engineering advancements that helped the new junior Lincoln bring buyers running were also found within the slabsided 1949 Mercury body. Big news, however, came beneath that curvaceous hood, where Mercurys were fitted with their own exclusive engine for the first time. Not a

Ford car or truck powerplant, this venerable "flathead" V8 featured a lengthened stroke that put output up to 255 cubic inches.

Introduced along with the all-new 1949 Fords and Lincolns, the 1949 Mercury was at first lost in the crowd, so to speak. Then along came James Dean, who drove a mildly customized 1949 Mercury in the 1955 movie *Rebel Without A Cause*. By the end of the decade, Mercury "lead sleds" were among California customizers' prime choices.

SPECIFICATIONS

Engine: *110-horsepower, 255 cubic-inch L-head V8*

Bore and stroke: *3.19 x 4.00 inches*

Compression: *6.8:1*

Fuel delivery: *Holley two-barrel carburetor*

Transmission: *three speed manual, standard; overdrive, optional*

Brakes: *hydraulic four-wheel drums*

Wheelbase: *118 inches*

Model availability: *two-door coupe, two-door convertible, four-dorr sport sedan and two-door station wagon*

Weight: *3,321 to 3,626 pounds*

Construction: *Body on frame*

Price: *$1,979 to $2,716*

Production: *301,319 all models*

1951-60: Rockin' & Rollin'

ABOVE: *V8 power, fins and chrome epitomize America's post-war self-confidence.*

"Ford still had considerable reason to celebrate during the 1950s, and not just because of skyrocketing sales. The company marked its 50th birthday in June 1953, and what a party it was."

The Fabulous Fifties brought us a lot of memorable things: Marilyn Monroe, rock 'n roll music, aluminum siding, suburban sprawl, and a world championship for baseball's beloved "bums," the Brooklyn Dodgers. Did we say Marilyn Monroe? This roller-coaster-ride of a decade also gave us Cold War sabre-rattling, police action in Korea, an economic recession, McCarthyism, and the Dodgers' detested defection west to California. Indeed, the 1950s could have been categorized as the best of times, as well as the worst.

In Ford's case the former was mostly true. Sure, the corporation did suffer through depressed economic times in 1958, but so did the rest of the industry. And who can forget the Edsel fiasco? Wags, stand-up comedians and that ilk still have not. Yet overshadowing these darker moments were so many bright, happy days that helped Henry Ford II and a couple of million car-buyers forget all about those less fortunate Forties.

Sales soared to all-new heights during the 1950s, predictably taking revenues along with them. The production tally in 1955 represented Ford's second highest ever, and those 1.4 million or so vehicles translated into a record $437 million in profits. Henry II's corporation firmly re-established itself as America's number two automaker during the 1950s, putting Chrysler back into third where it belonged. But Ford Division still could not quite catch up with Chevrolet in the low-priced rankings, though the race was tighter every year.

Photo finishes were the order of the day more than once, with a couple of calls remaining under further review by officials down on the field to this day. Both Chevrolet and Ford claimed top honors for what was one of Detroit's greatest years ever, so who cheated? Well, maybe Ford a little, as its 1957 model "year" actually ran for 13 months. When that extended period ended late in November, Dearborn officials claimed they'd built 1,674,488 cars in 1957. Chevrolet's 1957 model run, which lasted 12 typical months, produced a final

LEFT: *This prototype Thunderbird carries the sweeping fender embellishments of the Fairlane. They were deleted on production models.*

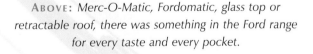

count of 1,515,177 coupes, sedans, station wagons and the rest. With all precincts in, Ford officials could not help but look across town for a concession speech.

Meanwhile their counterparts at Chevrolet were doing the same, and not because they were expecting a recount. Whether a 1957 Ford was sold in October 1956 or November 1957, it still counted the same, even if it was purchased in Palm Beach County, Florida. Discounting that extra month would not have made up the difference anyway, and there was not one chad—hanging, dimpled or otherwise—to be found anywhere.

What Chevrolet's paper-pushers did was reshuffle the stack. They concluded that their calendar-year production—cars built between January and December 1957—was 1,522,536,

ABOVE: *Merc-O-Matic, Fordomatic, glass top or retractable roof, there was something in the Ford range for every taste and every pocket.*

RIGHT:*The 1955 Fairlane Crown Victoria hardtop offered luxury cruising for $2200 and captures the youthful spirit of the decade perfectly.*

compared to Ford's comparable calendar-year total of 1,522,406. Bingo, Chevrolet was once more the big winner, if only by a marginal 130 Bel Airs, Corvettes and Nomads. How convenient; if the game does not end in your favor just find another scorekeeper. Differing tallies came into play again in 1959 when the two old rivals once more made conflicting claims to the coveted number one position.

Whatever the case, whatever the official finish, Ford still had considerable reason to celebrate during the 1950s, and not just because of skyrocketing sales. The company

ABOVE: *The Lincoln Capri was not intended, primarily, to be a "performance car", but there was more to it than met the eye. This is a 1954 Hardtop coupe.*

marked its 50th birthday in June 1953, and what a party it was. Festivities began with the "50th Anniversary Press Forum," held May 6-8 for journalists, who always seem to show whenever hoopla and hand-outs are involved. Dearborn's social chairmen then followed that up with special dinners for dealers across the country on June 17. In between, a Ford convertible had played the prestigious part of pace car at the 1953 Indy 500 and the company was honored on Ed Sullivan's weekly television program—which, by the way, was sponsored by Lincoln-Mercury.

Special events also included the May 7 formal dedication of the Ford Archives, which had actually opened near Greenfield Village back in 1951, and the ground-breaking ceremonies were held two weeks later for the new Research and Engineering Center, a facility that would begin operation in 1958. President Dwight Eisenhower was on hand with his shovel for the latter occasion.

On its actual anniversary, June 16, Ford reopened its Rotunda visitors center, closed since January 1942. And lest no one would forget why the Rotunda was back in the news on that day, party-throwers decorated it to look like an oversized birthday cake. Even bigger news came less than a week later as plans were announced for a new world headquarters in Dearborn, the so-called "Glass House." At the end of all the hubbub was Ford's gifts to its car-buyers—a 50th anniversary horn button on all 1953 models. Yippee.

Customers had considerably more to holler about the following year as Harold Youngren's engineers finally retired Henry's old flathead, replacing it with the modern overhead-valve "Y-block" V8, this came three years after Ford had previously introduced its first relatively modern automatic transmission. GM had beaten Ford to the punch with both an OHV V8 and an automatic transmission, but Dearborn in 1954

LEFT: *The "Sun Valley" glass roof option on the 1955 Fairlane crown Victoria might have proved uncomfortable on a sunny summer's day but would have been perfect for cruising beneath the stars.*

BELOW: The Carrera Panamerica, a viciously punishing road race through Mexico, was first run in 1950. A Lincoln Capri placed ninth—and a legend was born.

LEFT: Run over largely dirt roads, in searing heat, covering over 2000 miles, the Carrera Panamerica was a demanding test of man and machine. Lincolns regularly triumphed against the most exotic European opposition.

ABOVE: The Thunderbird gained a second row of seats in 1958, and its V8's power rose to 352 cubic inches.

did become the first to offer a low-priced car with innovative ball-joints, the work of chief engineer Earle MacPherson, in place of the antiquated, labor-intensive kingpins formerly used in front suspensions.

Designers in 1955 then followed all that technical talk up with one of the true automotive wonders of the 1950s, the two-seat Thunderbird. Styled by William Boyer under Frank Hershey's

ABOVE: *One thing that started the big move to Lincoln was the Capri's ability to outpace team Ferraris in the Carrera.*

artistic direction, this lovely little playtoy came about after Lewis Crusoe returned from the Paris Auto Show in 1951 with a head full of ideas; fun ideas based on the European sports car ideal. Though it was only built for three years, the two-place T-bird is still fondly remembered today and may well represent the most popular American automobile ever built.

With Thunderbirds jaunting about for barely a year, Dearborn officials made additional headlines in December 1955 by announcing that as many as 10.2 million shares of Ford Motor Company stock would be offered for sale to the public. That sale commenced on January 17, 1956, making Ford a public company for the first time since Henry had put his family in sole control back in 1919. Ford's first stockholders meeting in more than 35 years was gaveled to order on March 24.

About the same time, Henry Ford II chose to align his company with the Automobile Manufacturers Association, a move that would come back to haunt him one year

They'll know you've *arrived* when you drive up in an Edsel

1958 EDSEL

LEFT AND ABOVE: *Edsel Ford, Henry's beloved, first-born son, died before his time and so did the car named after him. There was nothing wrong with the Edsel, it just did not catch on...*

Ford

RIGHT: *Ford entered the four-by-four market before the term was coined. This monster dates from the late '1950s.*

later. During a meeting in May 1957 , AMA chairman Harlow "Red" Curtice proposed that the group's membership severe any and all ties with the racing community, a concession perhaps to the plain fact that Detroit's horsepower race, then in full gallop, had begun running harder and faster than safety allowed. All parties agreed, and on June 6 the AMA "ban" on factory racing was approved. From then on, member companies would "not

ABOVE: *Throughout the 1950s, the Truck division supplied the hardware to match the burgeoning highway system.*

"Though it was only built for three years, the two-place T-bird is still fondly remembered today and may well represent the most popular American automobile ever built."

participate or engage in any public contest, competitive event or test of a passenger car involving or suggesting racing or speed." They were also prohibited from advertising "the actual or comparative capabilities of passenger cars for speed, or the ability to accelerate or perform in any context that suggests speed." While Ford general manager Robert McNamara followed the resolution to the letter, other factories simply took their racing activities "underground." Chevrolets and Pontiacs continued running stronger than ever, at the track and on the street, after the AMA ban. Why?

It was no coincidence that the man behind the ban, Red Curtice, was also GM president. As luck would have it, the AMA action of June 1957 stopped Ford in its tracks (from a performance perspective) just as it was poised to overtake Chevrolet as America's number one automaker. And it would be another two or three years before someone in Dearborn began smelling a rat as high-performance components remained plentiful in GM parts books while hot hardware from Ford was all but non-existent. Among those who cried foul was a young Ford man on the go, Lee Iacocca.

1952-54 'Mexican Road Race' Lincoln

Commander Cody was referring to something totally different when he used to sing about the "Hot Rod Lincoln" that nearly drove his dad drinkin', but that lyrical label would fit Ford's luxury line during the early 1950s. From 1952 to 1954, Lincolns ran with the hottest stock-class race cars—as well as the world's.

Lincoln's prime proving ground then was the legendary Carrera Panamericana, the "Mexican Road Race," which covered nearly 2,000 tortuous miles up the Pan-American Highway from Tuxtla Gutierrez, near the Guatemalan border, north to Juarez, just across the Rio Grande from El Paso, Texas. First run in 1950, this savage competition was open to stock, factory-equipped vehicles from around the globe. In 1952 two classes, "sports" and "stock," were created, and these two were then each split into "large" and "small"

divisions for the 1953 race. "Special stock" and "European stock" were added in 1954, the event's last year.

Held in November 1952, the third Mexican Road Race served as a coming out for Lincoln's modernized 1953 models, hot on the heels of the division's radically redesigned 1952 Lincolns. News-making updates that year included a new X-member frame with bigger brakes and shocks and the industry's first ball-joint front suspension.

Power came from Lincoln's first modern overhead-valve short-stroke V8, which displaced 317 cubic inches and produced 160 warmly welcomed horses. Lincoln's first four-barrel carburetor then appeared in 1953 to help boost output for an improved 317 V8 to 205 horsepower. Once in the hands of West Coast hot rodders Bill Stroppe and Clay Smith, the aptly named "V-205" engine instantly became a force to be reckoned with down south of the border.

Stroppe and Smith were contracted by division officials to prepare a Lincoln team for the 1952 Carrera Panamericana. Each road-race Lincoln was treated to heavy-duty shocks and special scoops to deliver cooling air to the brakes, and the engines were balanced and blueprinted.

Lincolns dominated the event, taking the top four places in the stock class. Then the grease hit the fan. Three days later a rival team filed a protest claiming the Stroppe cars were "souped up" and did not qualify as "standard production" automobiles. Nonetheless, inspectors claimed that, after a "detailed and meticulous examination," the winning Lincolns were "within the specifications of the catalogue."

Lincolns claimed seven of the top nine positions in 1953 in what *The New York Times* called "the world's toughest race." Three drivers and four spectators were killed that year, and by 1954 the name had changed to "the world's most dangerous race."

Lincolns took the Mexican Road Race's top two spots in 1954 before the growing number of fatalities convinced officials to close the event down.

Thus ended the race career of the hot rod Lincoln.

SPECIFICATIONS

Engine: 317 cubic-inch OHV V8; 160 horsepower in 1952, 205 horsepower in 1953-54

Bore & stroke: 3.80 x 3.50 inches

Fuel delivery: Holley two-barrel carburetor in 1952; Holley four-barrel carburetor in 1953-54

Transmission: four-speed Hydra-Matic automatic supplied by GM

Brakes: hydraulic four-wheel drums

Suspension: independent control arms with ball joints and coils springs up front; longitudinal leaf springs and a solid axle in back

Price: ranged from $3,198 to $4,031

Wheelbase: 123 inches

Length: 214 inches in 1952-53; 215 inches in 1954

Weight: ranged from 4,125 pounds to 4,310

Model availability: two-door hardtop and four-door sedan in base Cosmopolitan series; two-door coupe, two-door convertible and four-door sedan in top-shelf Capri series

Construction: body on frame

Production: 27,001 for all models in 1952; 40,762 for all models in 1953; 36,993 for all models in 1954

1953 F-100 Pickup Truck

The postwar pickup truck market certainly was a busy place, with every competitor from Chevrolet on down to Studebaker working overtime trying to upstage the other. After both these two firms rolled out postwar all-new light-duty trucks in rapid fashion, Ford followed suit with its own new half-ton, the F-1, in 1948. But as impressive as the new F-series models were, they still were not quite capable of unseating Chevrolet as America's leading truckmaker. So Dearborn designers went back to the drawing board.

This time Ford reportedly spent $30 million on what probably represented Detroit's earliest use of an ergonomic study in a pickup truck design project. If it was not the earliest, it was surely the most comprehensive to that point. Driver and passenger comfort were the top priorities, as was ease of use. Stylists were also heavily involved, with the aim to balance form and function like no other pickup. The result was the renamed F-100, a milestone pickup if there ever was one.

When *Automobile* magazine named "The 24 Most Important Automobiles of the Century" in its September 1996 issue, included, along with Henry's first Model T, was the 1953 F-100. "Every comfortable, driver-friendly pickup on the road today owes its existence to the original Ford F-100," wrote *Automobile* founder David E. Davis, Jr. "Until the appearance of the restyled F-100 pickup, trucks were thought suitable only for commercial uses. But [this] was the first truck planned, styled and engineered by a corporate management team, and suddenly pickups became an alternative for personal transportation."

Ford advertising copy in 1953 claimed the new F-100 offered "more power, more comfort, more economy." Increased comfort was the result of the "Driver Engineered" cab, which among other things featured a wider seat with improved shock-absorbing capabilities, a steering wheel mounted at a better angle to reduce driver fatigue, and a larger, one-piece windshield that greatly increased visibility. According to *Mechanix Illustrated*'s Tom McCahill, the spacious three-passenger seat was "as comfortable as the average sedan's."

Among mechanical advancements was a redesigned chassis with its front axle relocated rearward for better balance and to reduce its turning radius (by 19 per cent). Also of note was an unprecedented choice of four transmissions: a synchromesh three-speed, a three-speed with overdrive, a four-speed with "grannie low," and the Ford-O-Matic automatic. The latter convenience option was a first for Ford's truck line and was only offered for half-ton F-series

pickups in 1953. The big boys still relied on "find-'em-and-grind-'em" manual gearboxes. Power sources were F-1 carryovers from 1952. F-100 pickups in 1953 could have been fitted with either the 215 cubic-inch overhead-valve six-cylinder or Ford's venerable "flathead" V8, which displaced 239 cubic inches that year.

The original F-100's career lasted four years, one less than the F-1's, an indication perhaps of the rapidly growing momentum of the 1950s pickup market. Upstaging the competition or catching up, it did not matter: the task grew tougher with each proceeding year. While the fabulous F-100 of 1953 did reverse a downward slide at Ford and broke a company sales record set in 1929, it too was incapable of helping Dearborn's truck team jump back ahead of Chevy's.

SPECIFICATIONS

Engine: *101-horsepower 215 cubic-inch OHV six-cylinder standard 110-horsepower 239 cubic-inch L-head V8 optional*

Price: *$1,330 (with base six-cylinder)*

Wheelbase: *110 inches*

Weight: *3,102 pounds*

Model availability: *two-door half-ton pickup truck*

Production: *116,437*

1955 Thunderbird 'Job One'

Among the many magazines to laud Ford for launching a new breed of American car in 1955 was *Sports Illustrated*, a new publication born right about the time the first Thunderbirds were beginning to roll down the Dearborn line. T-bird production began on September 9, 1954, with official sales opening October 22. Three weeks earlier, the October 4, edition of *Sports Illustrated* hit the stands with a three-page tribute to what *SI* editors called "America's newest Sports Car." According to this article, the car tested was "not a pilot model Thunderbird, but the number 1 production model."

Just think, the very first of 4.3 million Thunderbirds spanning 43 model runs. What a find that would be today, right? But what are the odds that the leader of this pack survived?

Not too long as far as George Watts was concerned. In August 1965, Watts, a devoted Thunderbird man from way back, came across a dilapidated 1955 T-bird parked outside a body shop in Santa Ana, California. As the story goes, its owner had dropped it off to have some work done but never came back to pick it up.

Stamped on the data plate beneath the hood were serial number 100005 and a build date code signifying September 9, 1954. Watts instantly recognized that he was looking at a Thunderbird assembled on the very first day of 1955 production. As for the serial number, 100,000 was typically Ford's starting point each year for each of its assembly lines. All vehicles rolling off those lines were then numbered consecutively from there. At first glance, Watts was sure he had discovered the earliest known Thunderbird. Too bad

this 'Bird had seen better days. "Everything about the car was either missing, broken, bent or dirty," claimed Watts in 1972. "But when I looked at the data plate and saw serial number 100005, the car took on a beautiful appearance. I knew it had to be one of the first five [T-birds] produced."

In truth, the news was even better than that. Wearing the 5th serial number for 1955 only meant that the vehicle in question was one of the first five Fords produced that year. A quick check of 1955 factory invoices in Dearborn revealed that serial numbers 100001 through

100004 indeed went to sedans or station wagons. Watts had not simply discovered the earliest 'Bird, he had found the first of the breed. On top of that, he took the historic wreck home for only $500. Three years later the historic two-seater was fully restored.

Eagle-eyed experts might notice a few idiosyncrasies in Watts' restoration. Up front, the headlight "brows" feature bright "Fairlane" trim, while the fender skirts in back are not trimmed out at all. Regular-production fender skirts for 1955 Thunderbirds were fitted with chrome moldings on their lower edges, and typical headlight bezels that year were plain with no trim.

Additional apparent discrepancies are found inside where there is no Thunderbird badge on the dashboard and no Ford "V8" crest on the glovebox door. Apparently some early 1955 Thunderbirds did come without the crest, but the rest got theirs directly below the glovebox latch. A few early 'Birds also appeared with the winged T-bird badge located down below the radio on the ashtray. The remaining cars, however, all proudly showed off their badges up high above the radio and maplight.

Engine: 198-horsepower 292 cubic-inch overhead-valve V8

Bore and Stroke: 3.75 x 3.30 inches

Compression: 8.5:1

Carburetor: single Holley four-barrel

Transmission: Ford-O-Matic automatic

Steering: worm and roller

Brakes: hydraulic four-wheel drums

Suspension: A-arms with coil springs up front; longitudinal leaf springs a solid rear axle in back

Price: $2,944

Wheelbase: 102 inches

Length: 175.3 inches

Height: 52.2 inches, with fiberglass hardtop in place

Width: 70.2 inches

Weight: 2,980 pounds

Model availability: two-door convertible with removable hardtop

Construction: body on X-member reinforced frame (with boxed side rails)

Production: 16,155

Performance: 0-60 mph in 9.5 seconds, quarter-mile in 16.9 seconds, according to March 1955 Road & Track

1956-57 Lincoln Continental Mk II

In January 1952 Ford's "Davis Committee" was formed to help formulate ideas on future product expansion. Headed by John Davis, who had been a part of the new Mercury launch 13 years earlier, the group quickly came up with two major recommendations, both of which looked promising at the start. The first involved the introduction of a new model line targeted for a niche just above Mercury. This line became Edsel. The second suggestion, also given an enthusiastic thumbs up from Henry Ford II's office, dealt with consumer demands for the return of the Lincoln Continental, which had last turned luxury buyers' heads in 1948.

Henry II's younger brother, William Clay Ford, then only 27, stepped up immediately in support of the latter project with hopes of creating America's ultimate luxury automobile. To this end, he was put in charge of the newly formed Special Product Operations group in July 1952. The name became Special Products Division in October 1953, then was changed again in April 1955—to Continental Division. Operating independently from Lincoln, this new division became home to one of the true classics of the postwar era, the Continental Mk II.

Not just a continuation of the Continental bloodline that ended in 1948, the Mk II represented the realization of some truly high ideals. To heck with bettering Cadillac, William Clay's target from the start was Rolls Royce. To reach this lofty goal, a veritable "all-star" team was gathered, including John Reinhart and Gordon Beuhrig. Put in charge of Mk II styling, Reinhart had formerly worked at GM, Packard and Raymond Loewy's cutting edge design studio. Beuhrig, the man behind the truly classic Cord 810/812 of 1936-37, was made chief body engineer. Chief engineer on the project was Harley Copp.

Announced in October 1954, the clean, crisp Continental Mk II was first shown publicly at the Paris Auto Show on October 6, 1955. Its official American introduction came in Dearborn on October 21 following various private showings given across the country from October 7-19. Advertisement teases included a television commercial shown during the *Ed Sullivan Show*.

At about $10,000, the Mk II was America's most expensive automobile. Nonetheless, buyers lined up eagerly in late 1955 and critics could not say enough about the reborn Continental. Calling the new Mk II "about the biggest thing that has happened in Detroit since the evolution of the Model A," *Car Life*'s G.M. Lightowler practically fell over himself in praise of this classic beauty. "Edsel Ford would be proud of his son Bill, the man most responsible for carrying this new Continental project through to its fabulous culmination. For the impact of this automobile will be felt in every country that makes automobiles. It will be felt also by every person who considers his car more than mere

transportation. Its simple distinctiveness of line and air of supreme elegance will be sought after by all who have an appreciation of quality and regality."

Such seekers were plentiful at first. The break-even point for Continental Division was 2,500 Mk II coupes a year, and roughly 1,200 were built during the last three months of 1955. Then the gleam almost immediately wore off. By January 1956 demand had dropped off to a point where dealers were now the ones doing the begging. Calendar-year Mk II production for 1956 was barely 1,300, and only 444 rolled off the line during the first five months of 1957, by which time the Division had reportedly lost $1,000 per car.

Enough was enough. Seeing the handwriting on the wall, corporate officials had closed down the Continental Division in July 1956. Then on May 8, 1957, official word came down to cancel the Mk II after only 3,000 were produced. Plain and simple, this modern classic was just too damned expensive, at least in Detroit terms. Clearly, building a Rolls was better left to the Brits.

SPECIFICATIONS

Engine: *368 cubic-inch OHV V8; 285 horsepower in 1956, 300 horsepower in 1957*

Bore & stroke: *4.00 x 3.66 inches*

Fuel delivery: *single four-barrel carburetor (Holley in 1956, Carter in 1967)*

Compression: *9.0:1*

Transmission: *Turbo-Drive three-speed automatic*

Brakes: *hydraulic four-wheel drums with power assist*

Steering: *re-circulating ball with power assist*

Suspension: *independent long/short arm with coils springs in front; longitudinal leaf springs with solid axle in back*

Price: *$9,695 in 1956; $9,966 in 1957*

Wheelbase: *126 inches*

Height: *56 inches*

Length: *218.4 inches*

Weight: *4,797 pounds in 1956; 4,825 in 1957*

Model availability: *two-door hardtop coupe (prototype convertibles were experimented with)*

Construction: *body on frame (frame was rugged ladder type with seven crossmembers and a central backbone running lengthwise in the middle)*

Production (calendar year): *1,231 in 1955; 1,325 in 1956; 444 in 1957*

1957 Ranchero

It is difficult to figure how Lee Iacocca could have later criticized Robert McNamara for being a conservative automobile executive considering the off-the-wall cars that appeared during his short watch in Dearborn. One, the 1957 Skyliner could actually transform from a hardtop into a convertible at the flick of a switch. And another hermaphrodite of sorts, the Ranchero, was both a car and truck at the same time. The ground-breaking Ranchero debuted in 1957, and it quickly changed the way Americans looked at utility vehicles.

Ranchero roots ran back 25 years and wrapped half way around the world. In the early 1930s, Ford of Australia had begun marketing its "Utility" roadster—"Ute" for short. This was a Ford automobile with cargo-bed bodywork incorporated in back, a practical combination that would roll on in popular fashion Down Under until 1958.

It was the Ute that undoubtedly inspired stylists back in Michigan to draw up a similar domestic model during the development stages for Ford's restyled 1952 line. Around Dearborn, this proposition became known as the "Roo Chaser." Planners at first rejected the idea, then along came McNamara in 1955. Ford's 1957 restyle was then in the works, presenting a wide-open opportunity for some truly creative interpretations of the 1950s ideal. Coupled with that was the fact that the first Ranchero was so easy to build.

Designers started with a 1957 two-door Ranch Wagon and basically cut off its roof at the back. The Ranchero and Ranch Wagon shared tailgates and rear compartment

subfloors. Unique to the former were the custom steel stampings for the cab roof, upper cab rear panel, the double-walled cargo box, the bed floor and the tailgate inner panel.

Described by Ford as "America's first work or play truck," the 1957 Ranchero was offered as a yeoman standard model and an upscale Custom. Though it was marketed as a half-ton pickup among the company's truck line, it clearly looked, as well as drove, an awful lot like a car. Save for heavier springing it was basically all Ford automobile beneath the skin. But that was not a bad thing.

As a pickup the Ranchero could haul upwards of 1,190 pounds in its 32.4 cubic-foot cargo box. As a car it could be dressed down with almost every comfort and convenience option offered by Ford in 1957.

Production of the first Ranchero hit 20,000, more than enough to convince Dearborn execs to keep it around for a while. The Ranchero remained in production until 1979, and along the way, it also inspired a copycat from Chevrolet, the El Camino.

The Ranchero experienced more than one transformation during its career. In 1960 it was reintroduced as a compact Falcon, which continued until 1966. It then became a Fairlane offering in 1967 as it jumped up a notch into Dearborn's intermediate ranks, where it would stay through evolutions as a Torino-based model (until 1977), followed by an LTD II variant for its last three renditions.

El Caminos outsold (by nearly a 2-1 margin) and outlasted their Ford counterparts, with Chevy's last car-truck leaving the line in 1988. But their can be only one "first of its kind," and that one was Ranchero.

SPECIFICATIONS

Engine: 223 cubic-inch L-head inline six-cylinder, standard
272 cubic-inch "Y-block" OHV V8, optional
292 cubic-inch "Y-block OHV V8, optional

Transmission: three-speed manual, standard; Ford-O-Matic automatic, optional

Wheelbase: 116 inches

Length: 202 inches

Width: 77 inches

Height: 57.2 inches

Weight: 3,520 pounds

Gross Vehicle Weight rating: 4,600 pounds

Price: $2,098 for base model; $2,149 for Custom

Model availability: two-door half-ton utility vehicle in base and Custom form

Construction: modified two station wagon body on standard passenger car ladder-type frame

Production: 21,695

1957 Mercury Turnpike Cruiser

Mercury was first chosen to be the prestigious pace car at the annual Indianapolis 500 in 1950. Not long afterward, that same car burst into flames while parked in front of Indy-winner Johnnie Parsons' home. A bad omen perhaps?

When the redesigned 1957 Mercury was named pace car for the 41st Indy 500, it was also announced that a new procedure would be put in place to start the race. Two pace laps instead of one would be run that May. The field of 33 cars would leave the newly constructed pit lane single-file behind the pacer and do a "parade lap" while forming up into the traditional 11 rows of three. Hopefully the drivers then would have the proper formation in place in time for the second go-around, the actual pace lap.

So much for best-laid plans. During the tussle to form up, drivers Eddie Russo and Elmer George collided, eliminating their machines

before the race even began. Was it mere coincidence that Mercury was not invited back to The Brickyard for nearly 10 years? But seriously, folks, the droptop that paced the 1957 Indy 500 had nothing to do with the pre-race accident—that is unless Russo and George had been caught gawking at Mercury's ostentatious display of Fifties-flair-gone-

haywire when they should have been finding their place in the field.

Who could have blamed them? The long, low and wide ragtop at the head of the pack that year was the new Turnpike Cruiser, a specially trimmed, chrome-encrusted rendition of an all-new body that was already "busy" enough in base form with its pronounced headlight brows, huge bumpers and "flying-V" taillights. Mercury men dubbed it "Dream

as were twin air intakes at each front corner of the roof, an expansive "Skylight Dual-Curve Windshield" that wrapped up into the top as well as around the sides, and a retractable, power-operated "Breezeway Ventilation" window in back housed beneath a rear-roof overhang section.

A Turnpike Cruiser convertible came along once Mercury was chosen to pace the 500. While this variety lost all that extra "flair" on top, it did receive a "Continental kit" spare tire carrier in back that added even more length to a road-going showboat that was as long as your old uncle Elmo's bar tab to begin with. Turnpike Cruisers were also fitted with Lincoln's 368 cubic-inch V8, a 290-horse-

power engine that was optional on other Mercs that year. And the "Convertible Cruiser" also could have been dressed up in pace car replica garb to allow Mercury buyers a chance to pretend they were running the lead lap at Indy.

Car Design," while *Mechanix Illustrated* scribe Tom McCahill called it "Space Age Design for Earth Travel."

First offered in two- and four-door hardtop form, the 1957 Turnpike Cruiser added even more flamboyance. Glaring quad headlights were standard,

Any traffic accidents occurring during these daydreams were not the responsibility of Mercury Division or any representative thereof.

1957-59 Ford Skyliner 'Retractable'

Ever Detroit's styling leader during the 1950s, General Motors once again wowed the masses with the first of its popular "pillarless hardtop convertibles" in 1949, establishing yet another trend for the rest of the automaking world to follow. This attractive new design fad featured a full-roofed car that at least looked like a convertible thanks to its light and airy roofline, which was devoid of the "pillar" typically found behind the door on a sedan. But as Ford stylist Gilbert Spear asked, "how can it be a 'hardtop convertible' if the top doesn't go down?"

Spear answered his own question with a design based on the premise that no idea is too fantastic as long as someone will buy it. Others had tried this "retractable hardtop" idea before—Tucker-designer Alex Tremulis' innovative Thunderbolt showcar, built by Chrysler in 1939, stands out most prominently from an American perspective. But it was Spear who managed the greatest success mating weather-proof transportation with wind-in-your-hair excitement.

William Clay Ford, head of Ford's Special Projects Division, was so impressed by Spear's initial sketches in 1953 he approved $2.2 million worth of development work. William saw a future for a Continental Mark II "Retractable," and in July 1953 he gave ex-GM engineer Ben Smith 18 months to make the dream into a reality. Though Smith and crew did manage to build a working prototype based on a 1952 Lincoln, by 1955 upper management had decided the returns could not justify the costs—the limited-production Mark II would only be offered in one bodystyle, with a fixed roof. However, with more than $2 million already spent,

Dearborn officials certainly were not going to pitch Spear's idea. Another $18 later, the Retractable re-appeared, this time as part of the higher-volume Ford Division passenger-car line. Though given less than a year to adapt the design to the smaller chassis, engineers came through, producing a 1957 Retractable prototype for a New York Auto Show introduction on December 8, 1956. On April 14, 1957, Ford's first Retractable Skyliner—the latter name taken from the equally inventive glass-top Crown Victorias of 1954-56—was delivered to President Eisenhower. Selected dealers received a limited number of Skyliners later that month and regular production picked up soon afterward. In all, 20,766 Retractables were sold in 1957, an impressive figure considering the model was on sale for a mere five months.

At $2,945, the 1957 Skyliner sold for $455 less than the 1957 Thunderbird and $340 more than the conventional 1957 Sunliner convertible. For that extra cash, a Skyliner buyer got the same open-air thrills a Sunliner owner enjoyed with an intriguing sideshow thrown in as part of the deal. *LIFE* magazine called it "the birth of a mechanical miracle… the most exciting idea in automobile design since Ford presented the first two-door sedan in 1915."

As 1950s fads went, the Retractable was certainly a success, at least during that first year. But once the gimmicky appeal wore off, sales started dropping, albeit slowly. Ford officials kept the act going for three years before closing it down. Various other retractable hardtop models have surfaced since from both foreign and domestic producers. Most notable in 2003 is Chevrolet's new SSR pickup truck, a limited-use toy that makes Ford's Skyliners of 1957-59 look like purely practical transports.

SPECIFICATIONS

Engine: OHV V8 in various displacements
272 cubic inches in 1957 standard; 292 and 312 cubic inches optional 292 cubic inches in 1958 & '59, standard; 332 and 352 cubic inches optional

Transmission: three-speed manual, standard; Fordomatic, optional; three-speed Cruise-O-Matic automatic, optional in 1958-59

Steering: worm and gear

Brakes: four-wheel hydraulic drums

Suspension: upper & lower control arms with coil springs in front; longitudinal leaf springs in back

Price: $2,942 in 1957; $3,138 in 1958; $3,346 in 1959

Wheelbase: 118 inches

Weight: 3,916 pounds in 1957; 4,069 in 1958; 4,064 pounds in 1959

Model availability: two-door convertible with retractable hardtop roof

Construction: body on frame

Production: 20,766 in 1957, 14,713 in 1958, 12,916 in 1959

1958-60 Edsel

In development since 1954 or so, Ford's long-rumored "E-car" was being readied for its introduction as a 1958 model and its moniker remained undetermined. Thousands of titles were considered before it was named "Edsel," a supposed honor that Henry Ford II and the rest of the family opposed at first. But board chairman Ernie Breech prevailed: Henry II gave in to Breech's pleas and allowed the all-new medium-priced model line to be named after his father.

Still the butt of an occasional joke today, the Edsel only managed to dishonor a figure who deserved so much better. Always trapped beneath old Henry's thumb, Edsel Ford never really made his own mark, and the achievements he did manage rarely garner anywhere near the respect given to lesser automotive milestones. Whatever chance he had at being remembered for his greatest

moments (Mercury; Lincoln KB, Zephyr and Continental), basically went away once people began associating his name with one of America's most renown business failures.

The car itself was not really that bad. Okay, maybe its styling did deserve a sling or arrow or two; perhaps the most famous reflection from the wag set concerning the 1958 Edsel was that it looked like an "Oldsmobile sucking a lemon." And maybe product planners did mess-

up by placing the Edsel so close to the existing Mercury line price-wise. Sales of the slightly less expensive Mercurys cut into the Edsel's prospects, which were damaged even further by the simultaneous arrival of a national recession in 1958.

Plain and simple, Ford's timing sucked, and that in itself represents blame enough for the Edsel's failure. Just a few years before, American car-buyers had been clamoring for more of everything: more chrome, more gadgets, more car. Then once cash got tight in 1958, much of the market's attention turned to smaller, affordable transports, like American Motor's new

Rambler and Studebaker's Lark. Undoubtedly no new car with the stature and prestige Edsel had to offer would have gotten off the ground then. As one Ford exec quipped, "It was a car right on target, only the target moved."

Had other corporate officials owned crystal balls, they would have killed the Edsel right then and there after 1958 sales fell well short of the company's publicized expectations. The play then became a comedy after 1959's performance drew far worse returns, and most critics nowadays do not even remember the few built for 1960.

Earlier models have not been so fortunate. Those first Edsels remain in the public eye some 40 years after the fact—for all the wrong reasons.

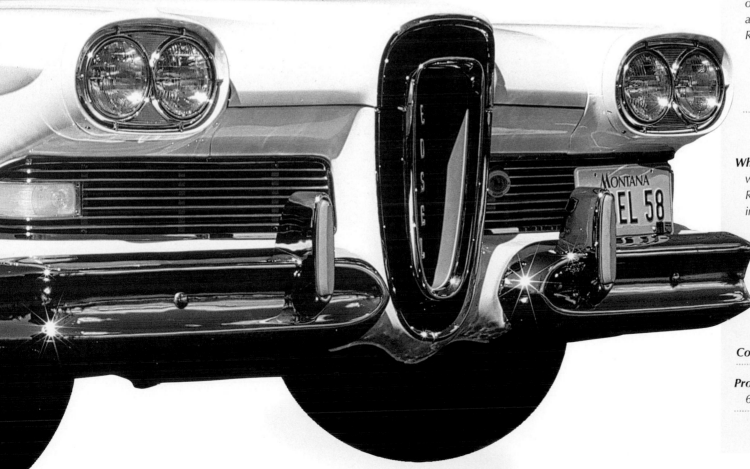

SPECIFICATIONS

Engine: *361 cubic-inch OHV V8, standard for Ranger/Pacer in 1958 410 cubic-inch OHV V8 standard for Corsair/Citation in 1958 292 cubic-inch OHV V8 standard for Ranger and station wagons in 1959 223 cubic-inch inline six-cylinder optional for Ranger/wagons in 1959 332 cubic-inch OHV V8 standard for Corsair in 1959 361 cubic-inch OHV V8 optional for all Edsels in 1959 292 cubic-inch OHV V8 standard for all Edsels in 1960 223 cubic-inch inline six-cylinder and 361 cubic-inch OHV V8 optional for all Edsels in 1960*

Transmission: *three-speed manual standard for Ranger/Pacer in 1958; Tele-Touch automatic standard for Corsair/Citation in 1958; three-speed manual standard for all Edsels in 1959; overdrive, two-speed Mile-O-Matic automatic, and three-speed Dual-Range Mile-O-Matic automatic, optional in 1959; three-speed manual standard for all Edsels in 1960, two- and three-speed automatics optional in 1960*

Price: *ranged from $2,375 to $3,801*

Wheelbase: *116 inches for station wagons in 1958; 118 inches for Ranger/Pacer series in 1958; 124 inches for Corsair/Citation in 1958; 120 inches for all 1959 and 1960 Edsels*

Weight: *ranged from 3,601 pounds to 4,311 pounds*

Model availability: *numerous*

Construction: *body on frame*

Production (all models): *1958, 63,110; 1959, 44,891; 1860, 2,846*

1961-70: The Total Performance Years

"bean counters [have] impressive analytical skills, [but] by their very nature, tend to be defensive, conservative and pessimistic. On the other side are the guys in sales and marketing— aggressive, speculative and optimistic. In any company, you need both."

Former Whiz Kid Robert McNamara became Ford Division general manager in 1955, a great year for the company, as well as the entire auto industry. Various definitely interesting vehicles debuted during his tenure, including the "Retractable" Skyliner and Ranchero, both in 1957, and the long-running Galaxie in 1959. That big showboat was followed up by Ford's first compact, the Falcon, introduced in late 1959, as a 1960 model. Appearing just as import sales were reaching all-new heights in the U.S., the Falcon was the right car for the right time, a claim supported by record first-year sales of more than 400,000.

McNamara was rewarded for such success with a promotion to Ford president in November 1960. But he was barely in office a month or so before newly elected U.S. president John Kennedy made him his Secretary of Defense. John Dykstra briefly held the Ford presidency before another Whiz Kid, Arjay Miller, took over in 1963.

As for McNamara's former post at Ford Division, that gap was filled back in November 1960 by the company's youngest general manager ever, 36-year-old Lee Iacocca, a mover and shaker if there ever was one. Iacocca had watched as McNamara had made his mark with the frugal Falcon, but he was not entirely impressed— with man or car. "[McNamara] was a good businessman, but he had the mentality of a consumerist," wrote Iacocca in his 1984 autobiography. "He believed strongly in the idea of a utilitarian car, whose purpose was simply to meet people's basic needs."

Iacocca, on the other hand, saw a better way to appeal to car buyers, especially the younger, livelier ones. This target market would soon be ballooning to unprecedented proportions thanks to the "baby boom" created after millions of lonely military men had returned home to their wives at the end of World War II. In Iacocca's humble opinion, McNamara's legacy would surely fall flat in the face of this youthful onslaught. What worked in the 1950s simply would not wash in the new decade, basically because Ford then had paid too much attention to the bottom line when they should have been speculating in automotive futures.

According to the new general manager, his predecessor "was the quintessential bean counter." "At their best," continued Iacocca,

LEFT: *Workers at the Kar Kraft plant prepare to shoe-horn a "Cobra-Jet"429 cubic inches, aluminum head, 370bhp V8 into a 1969 Boss Mustang.*

BELOW: "Father of the Mustang" Lee A. Iacocca (left) is pictured with Donald Frey, Ford's Chief Engineer and the Mustang's original product manager, as they survey their handiwork: the 1964 original.

"bean counters [have] impressive analytical skills, [but] by their very nature, tend to be defensive, conservative and pessimistic. On the other side are the guys in sales and marketing—aggressive, speculative and optimistic. In any company, you need both sides, because natural tension between the two creates its own system of checks and balances. If the bean counters are too weak, the company will spend itself into bankruptcy. But if they're too strong, the company won't meet the market or stay competitive."

Among other things, Iacocca and others at Ford felt the company was

BELOW: *John Holman and Ralph Moddy do some seriously heavy breathing on a 289 V8 back in 1966.*

not staying competitive thanks to McNamara's adherence to the AMA anti-performance edict, a "paper tiger" that GM executives all but ignored. As the old adage goes, speed sells, a plain fact not missed by another young general managers in Detroit, Semon E. "Bunkie" Knudsen, son of William Knudsen, the man who had jumped ship at Ford back in the 1920s to help Chevrolet rise to the forefront.

In 1956, Bunkie Knudsen had taken the reins at Pontiac and almost instantly transformed that tired GM division into a builder of true excitement. Winning races and maximizing performance were among the keys to Pontiac's turnaround during the late-1950s, this despite the AMA decision against such shenanigans. Ban or no ban, Bunkie knew he had to appeal to a younger crowd, and hot hardware represented the easiest enticement as far as this group was concerned. "You can sell a young man's car to an old man," went his prime motto, "but you'll never sell an old man's car to a young man."

RIGHT: *The 1966 289 cubic inch. "High Performance" V8 had a bore and stroke of 4.00 x 2.87 inches and could develop up to 271 bhp, but much more was to come....*

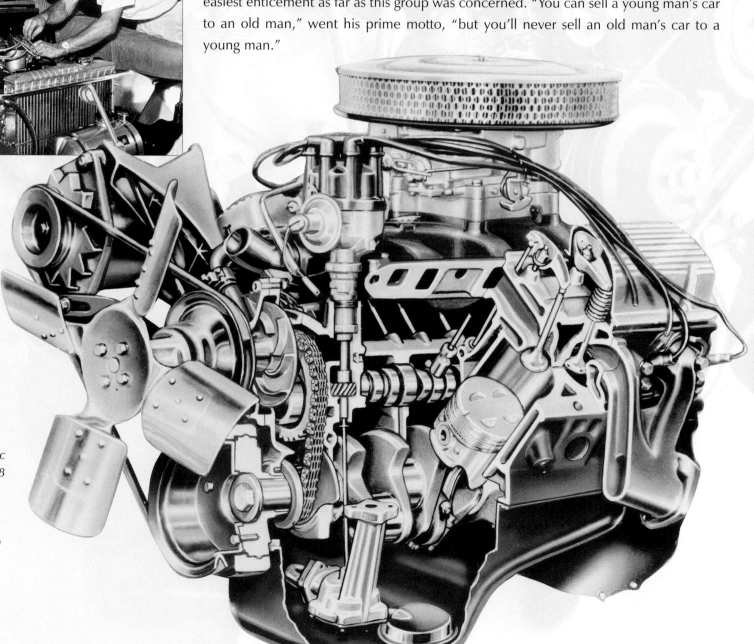

"You can sell a young man's car to an old man," went Bunkie Knudsen's prime motto, "but you'll never sell an old man's car to a young man."

ABOVE: *The 1969 Boss 302 packed just short of 300bhp of punch and retailed at just over $3,500, 1,934 were produced, against 858 of the mighty 429s. The late 1960s were the heyday of the Pony Car and the Mustang was THE Pony Car.*

Iacocca too recognized the same reality, as did Henry Ford II after he watched Ford fall well behind its rivals in Detroit's ever-present horsepower race. In April 1959, Henry II's office had sent a letter to GM officials detailing Ford's plans to begin offering high-performance options again. Also mentioned was a possible revamping of the AMA agreement. There was no reply, so Ford executives simply began doing what their Chevrolet and Pontiac counterparts had been doing all along—race like there was no tomorrow. Three years later, in June 1962, Henry Ford II made it official: in his opinion, the AMA edict was history.

"Performance has been integral in the long history of the Ford Motor Company. We believe in performance, because the search for performance—Total Performance—made the auto-mobile the wonderfully efficient, pleasurable machine it is today—and will make it better tomorrow."

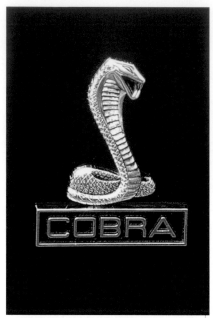

By then Ford had become a major player at various racing venues, not the least of which was NASCAR's stock-car circuit. Big, brawny engines with outputs surpassing 400 horsepower were finding their ways beneath Ford hoods by 1961, the same year the company's first full-sized "four-on-the-floor" model was offered. Next came Iacocca's announcement in April 1963 of his exciting "Total Performance" campaign. What was "Total Performance?"

"[It] literally is hundred of things that let you control an automobile more safely and cover ground more swiftly," he said. "Performance has been integral in the long history of the Ford Motor Company. We at Ford believe in performance, because the search for performance—Total Performance—made the auto-mobile the wonderfully efficient, pleasurable machine it is today—and will make it better tomorrow."

Truly, Ford performance reached all-new highs during the 1960s, at least on the race track. By 1965, Dearborn had teamed up with the Holman-Moody race shop in North Carolina and Carroll Shelby's Shelby American firm, in California, to produce some of the most outrageous factory-backed competition machines the world had ever scene. Stock-car racing, drag-racing, road-racing, even the Indianapolis 500—everywhere you looked there seemed to be a Blue Oval in the

winner's circle. Then came Henry Ford's grand glory: a win at the 24 Hours of Le Mans in 1966 to secure his Ford's reputation as the world's most competitive car company.

On the street, however, it was another story, as Total Performance did not quite translate so well for the average car-buyer. Sure, Iacocca did turn everyone's heads with his exciting new Mustang in 1964, but that mass-market marvel was not necessarily a high-performance car. Although hot options were available, most Mustangs were affordable, practical compacts that only looked and felt sporty, a fact revealed quite prominently after Chevrolet and Pontiac introduced their own "ponycars" for 1967. Camaros and Firebirds in top performance trim made Mustangs look feeble, at least until the fabled 428 Cobra Jet model debuted in April 1968.

A long list of so-called "musclecars" followed immediately after the Cobra Jet Mustang hit the ground running that year, primarily because of a change in command at Ford. In February 1968, Henry Ford II had shocked everyone in Detroit by making Bunkie Knudsen president of Ford Motor Company; this after Bunkie had resigned in a tizzy because Ed Cole was made GM president instead of him. Left aghast by the decision was Iacocca, who had every reason to be upset after he himself was passed over. He even briefly considered doing to Ford what Bunkie had done to GM, but then he decided to stick around and watch. He made the right choice.

"Henry was a great GM admirer," recalled Iacocca. "For him, Knudsen was a gift from heaven. Perhaps he believed Knudsen had all that famous GM wisdom locked in his genes." Maybe so, but that was not necessarily a good thing as office politics worked drastically different at the two big corporations, and the GM defector wasted little time stepping on toes everywhere he went in Dearborn.

ABOVE: *A Shelby Cobra leads a Shelby Daytona coupe through a left-hander on a tight and twisting English circuit in the late 1960s.*

RIGHT: *A driver's eye view of the subsidiary instrument cluster in Mercury's 1965 Comet Cyclone coupe.*

OPPOSITE PAGE: *Carroll Shelby first crammed a 260 cubic inch, Ford V8 into an English AC Ace chassis in 1962, thereby creating the legendary Cobra. These cars, in 427 form, became invincible in competition, rivaled only by the Corvette Gran Sports that were specially produced to challenge them...*

Along with that, Knudsen kept pushing Ford products in a direction contrary to changing attitudes. The big, bad Boss 302 and Boss 429 Mustangs were his babies, and he also okayed the upcoming 1971 Mustang redesign that enlarged the car considerably to make room for more engine and even higher performance. "When

Six and the single girl.

What makes a quiet, sensible girl like Joan fall in love with a Mustang? Not simply Mustang's steely good looks or smooth, racy lines. Not even the hard-to-resist features like adjustable bucket seats, wall-to-wall carpeting, sports steering wheel, and floor-mounted shift.

What really broke down Joan's reserve was the solid practicality of Mustang's deep breathing Six. She knew she could trust this husky, suave brute of an engine to squire her around town, drive her to the mountains for a weekend, even drop her off for dinner with the girls (who will never guess how little Mustang costs her to own and run). Extraordinarily considerate of a girl's feelings... and her pocketbook.

Take a test drive and see if you should give in to Mustang because of sheer Six appeal. Smart girls do.

MUSTANG
Ford

ABOVE: *The Mustang's base motor, from its launch in 1965, was to prove reliable; a 170 cubic inches straight-six from the Falcon, bored and stroked to 200 cubic inches to provide 120 bhp, which was considered sufficient power for the girls, in those days.*

By 1970, performance was considered unsafe and a major threat to the air that we breathe. Musclecars had also grown too expensive to buy and insure, and soon they would be too expensive to operate once gas prices began to soar in the 1970s.

Mr. Knudsen came from GM, he brought along a strong belief in the power of performance," wrote *Motor Trend*'s Eric Dahlquist.

Yet by then the days of big engines and high horsepower were all but over. The musclecar was history. Safety crusaders, insurance agents and tailpipe sniffers had seen to that. Seemingly everyone in Detroit in the late-1960s knew an end of era was upon them except for Bunkie. "He was a racing nut, but he failed to understand that the heyday of racing had passed," said Iacocca.

He also failed to heed Henry Ford II's warnings about his aggressive ways, a mistake that finally cost him his job in September 1969. Though some claimed Knudsen was trying to take over, Iacocca had another explanation for the short-term president's quick demise: "I wish I could say Bunkie got fired because his ideas were all wrong. But the actual reason was because he used to walk into Henry's office without knocking. That's right—without knocking!"

With Knudsen knocked out, Iacocca then helped fill the void along with two other executives in a "trioka" arrangement. Finally, on December 10, 1970, he was made the lone president. Fortunately he chose to stay at Ford and watch Knudsen fail, a result that he was not alone in rooting for. "The day Bunkie was fired there was great rejoicing and much drinking of champagne," he remembered. "Over in public relations, one of our people coined a phrase that soon became famous throughout the company: 'Henry Ford once said that history is bunk. But today, Bunkie is history.'"

So too was Ford's far-flung racing empire. On November 20, 1970, Ford Motor Company sales group vice president Matthew McLaughlin announced that Dearborn was pulling out of nearly all motorsport activities. "The greatest peacetime nongovernmental competitive effort to occur in this century has quietly drawn to a close—the victim of progress," noted *Motor Trend*'s Jim Brokaw.

In 1960 Iacocca had begun pushing Ford to jump on the youth market bandwagon. Ten years later, the members of that market were older and wiser, and the sales-conscious marketing man was paying close attention to changing attitudes. By 1970, performance was considered unsafe and a major threat to the air that we breathe. Musclecars had also grown too expensive to buy and insure, and soon they would be too expensive to operate once gas prices began to soar in the 1970s. Racing, too, had become a bad investment. "It's no secret that Iacocca questions the value returned for each racing dollar [spent]," announced a report in *Motor Trend*, January 1971. "It is also no secret that deposed former president Bunkie Knudsen was a staunch supporter of racing, and anything that was in to Bunkie is currently out."

A new concern, cleaning up the environment, had become the top priority at Ford as the 1960s wound down. "In 1969, Henry II pledged the assets of the company to help whip the pollution problem," wrote Brokaw. "He wasn't fooling. Shortly after his speech, Ford announced the allocation of $18 million for the installation of anti-smoke equipment on the factories' smoke stacks. Two months later, the racing budget for 1970 was drastically reduced by about 75 per cent."

"The days of big engines and high horsepower were all but over. The musclecar was history. Safety crusaders, insurance agents and tailpipe sniffers had seen to that".

RIGHT: *The first Mustang Shelby Cobra GT 350s and GT 500s roll towards completion at the Smith Plastics plant in Ionia, Michigan.*

BELOW: *The 1960 Thunderbird convertible weighed in at close to 4,000 pounds. Fitted with a 430 cubic inch V8, it was heavy on fuel, too.*

1960 Falcon

Small cars were certainly nothing new in this country when the Big Three jumped onto the compact bandwagon late in 1959. Crosley, Kaiser-Frazer, Hudson and Nash all had tried introducing Americans to radically downsized, affordable, economical transportation first dating back to just before WW II. A world war prior to that, the cyclecar craze had swept the U.S. enticing entry-level buyers into the market with lightweight machines that indeed were not much more than a couple of bikes bolted together with an engine in between.

Let us not forget the import invasion, which came first from Europe after peace returned to this planet, however briefly, in 1946. Most prominent among these pesky little interlopers was Germany's Volkswagen, the beloved "Beetle," the compact creation that eventually topped the Model T to become the world's all-time best-selling car. On its own, the popular VW was enough to inspire Detroit execs to start thinking small.

That they did. GM, Chrysler and Ford all introduced compact

models for 1960, Dearborn being the first to show its competitor off to the press in July 1959. Of this trio, Chevrolet's rear-engined, air-cooled Corvair was the most radical engineering-wise. Chrysler's Valiant perhaps was the most radically styled, and Ford's Falcon was the best seller.

Initially conceived as the "XK Thunderbird" project in 1957, the Falcon featured unitized body-frame construction, a short 109-inch wheelbase and a tidy base price beginning right around $1,900. Ford's new 144 cubic-inch six-cylinder engine supplied more than enough horses (90) to get this little machine rolling while at the same time promising frugal fuel economy of about 27 miles per gallon.

"Similar in size and general concept to the [American Motors] Rambler and [Studebaker] Lark, Ford's tactical approach to the [small car] skirmish carries the weight of simmered-down flashiness, guaranteed economy, and realistically comfortable seating space, stressing 'cost of ownership' as the major selling point," claimed *Motor Trend*'s October 1959 cover story on what many felt represented the biggest news out of Dearborn in about 30 years. "Not since the days of the Model A has Ford concentrated on functional styling and engineering as part and parcel of what it thinks the American car-buying public wants," continued *Motor Trend*'s Steve DaCosta.

Included in the first Falcon's model lineup was both a two- and four-door station wagon and Dearborn's latest variation of its "car-truck" Ranchero. Falcon-based Rancheros were offered up through 1966. Simple sportiness showed up in 1961 in the form of the bucket-seat-equipped Falcon Futura, which was then topped by an even sportier V8-powered Falcon Sprint mid-year in 1963.

Base Falcons themselves evolved into bigger, better-equipped small cars as the 1960s progressed, and popularity started to sag as they did. Sales dropped so low in 1970 that officials decided to delete the original compact ideal mid-year and transferred the Falcon badge up into the intermediate Fairlane ranks. Both the Fairlane and Falcon nameplates were themselves deep-sized at the end of the year. But by then another headline-making small car, the Pinto, had appeared to pick up where the original Falcon had left off a few years before.

SPECIFICATIONS

Engine: 90-horsepower 144 cubic-inch OHV inline six-cylinder

Bore & stroke: 3.50 x 2.50 inches

Compression: 8.7:1

Fuel delivery: Holley one-barrel carburetor

Transmission: three-speed manual, standard; automatic, optional

Suspension: independent upper/lower control arms with coil springs, front; longitudinal leaf springs and solid axle in back

Price: ranged from $1,912 to $2,287

Wheelbase: 109.5 inches

Length: 181.2 inches

Weight: ranged from 2,317 to 2,570

Model availability: four-door sedan, two-door sedan, four- and two-door station wagon, two-door Ranchero (marketed in the truck line)

Construction: unitized body/frame

Production: 435,676 for all models except Ranchero

1961 Lincoln Continental convertible

Four-door phaetons—convertibles to us today—were a relatively common sight before World War II. They were even more so around World War I when open-air travel basically represented the only way to fly. But all that started to change once easier, cheaper ways to manufacture full-roofed car bodies were found.

The Continental convertible represented a great combination of youthful excitement and all the comfort, convenience and class Lincoln could offer. It was also a timeless classic in the looks department and an engineering marvel beneath that beautiful skin.

Chief engineer Harold MacDonald's idea guys handled the nuts and bolts. They helped replace the ostentatious monstrosities left over from the 1950s with a beautifully understated boulevard cruiser

compact 123-inch wheelbase was eight inches shorter than its 1960 predecessor. Overall length shrank by 14.6 inches, yet curb weight remained almost unchanged at about 5,000 pounds.

How did less end up being almost more? When used on compacts, unitized construction then usually meant equal strength with less weight compared to conventional body-on-frame designs. But when this technique was applied to a larger luxury car, the weight kept piling on as the body was re-enforced to guarantee a quiet, sure ride. By the

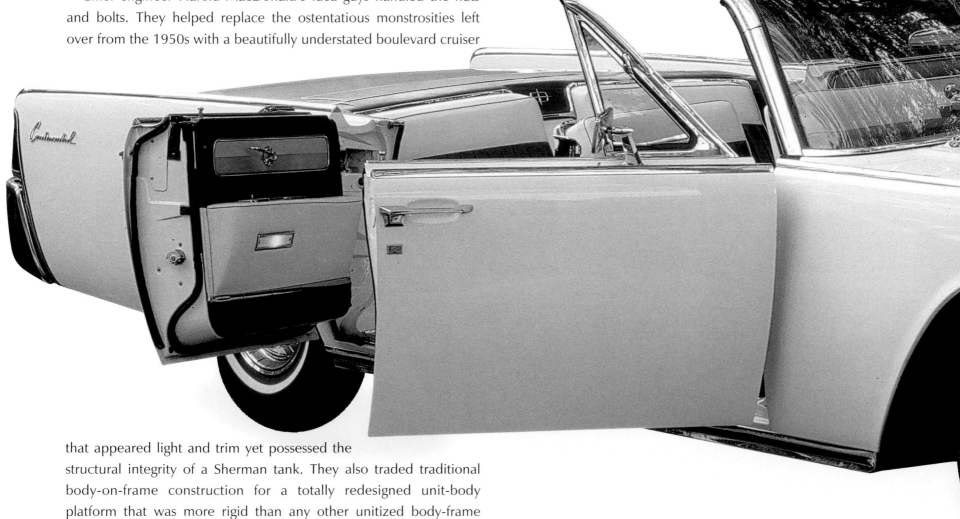

that appeared light and trim yet possessed the structural integrity of a Sherman tank. They also traded traditional body-on-frame construction for a totally redesigned unit-body platform that was more rigid than any other unitized body-frame construction ever seen. The 1961 Continental had 67 per cent more torsional rigidity than its massive forerunner, it was also just as heavy, even though various dimensions were reduced. The newest Lincoln's

time engineers worked out the kinks, the 1961 Lincoln was one of the tightest, heaviest ships out of Detroit.

It was the "tightness" that allowed Lincoln designers to build the four-door convertible. With or without a steel roof, torsional rigidity of the Lincoln unibody was the same. All conventional convertibles required extra chassis re-enforcement to make up for the rigidity lost when a hardtop is converted into a ragtop. This translates into added weight and expense. Relatively speaking, the Lincoln convertible gained very little compared to its four-door sedan running mate— 200 pounds of semi-intricate top mechanism and 100 pounds of "tuning weight" placed at the car's four corners to cancel out harmonic vibrations at speed.

This was a car that all involved knew would not be a major seller, but one that would be more than worth its weight in heads turned. Credit went to Ford designers: Gene Bordinat, Elwood Engel, Don DeLaRossa, John Najjar, Gail Halderman, and Robert Thomas, who worked under styling vice-president, George Walker. It was Engel's advanced studio that deserved the most kudoes for the clean, crisp body that originally began life as a Thunderbird proposal. It looked so good, however, that Ford president Robert McNamara could not resist promoting the design into the top-line Lincoln ranks. The final product was then honored by the Industrial Designers Institute as "an outstanding contribution of simplicity and design elegance." More than 40 years later the Lincoln Continental convertible still looks like a million bucks.

SPECIFICATIONS

Engine: *300-horsepower, 430 cubic-inch overhead-valve V8*

Compression: *10:1*

Bore and Stroke: *4.30 x 3.70 inches*

Fuel delivery: *single Carter two-barrel carburetor*

Transmission: *Turbo-Drive automatic*

Price: *$6,713*

Wheelbase: *123 inches*

Overall length: *212.4 inches*

Width: *78.6 inches*

Weight: *4,594 pounds*

Model availability: *four-door convertible*

Production: *2,857*

1962-63 Thunderbird Sports Roadster

Ford called it a roadster, although it really was not. Roll-up windows technically disqualified this vehicle from that category. Misnomers or not, the Thunderbird Sports Roadsters of 1962 and 1963 were by no means imposters. In truth, this exciting, not-so-small two-seater probably defined its own niche—which was not without precedent in the T-bird legacy.

Americans had seen nothing else like it when that first little two-seat 'Bird debuted in September 1954. Sporty, sexy, status-laden; you name it, the 1955 Thunderbird fitted the bill. As did the 1956 model, and the 1957. Then came the marketing move that horrified the purists. Adding a backseat for 1958 may have guaranteed survival of the species, but many felt Ford stopped building real Thunderbirds after 1957. Their complaints could still be heard three years later when a rounder, restyled Thunderbird debuted for 1961.

But curiously enough those protests did not fall on deaf ears. As early as 1960, work had begun on a new type of two-seat T-bird thanks to car marketing manager Lee Iacocca, who had been bombarded with requests from dealers—themselves well aware of purists demands for a return to the good ol' days—to bring back the two-seat T-bird. Of course redesigning the Thunderbird minus that other seat in back was out of the question; no amount of moaning and groaning would change that fact. On the other hand, inspiration for a revival of true personal luxury already existed.

Quick-thinking entrepreneurs had begun experimenting with two-place conversion using rear-seat tonneau covers almost immediately after the 1958 Thunderbird had appeared. Perhaps the first came from New Jersey Ford dealer Bill Both, who also happened to own a fiberglass fabrication business. Booth commissioned his men to fashion just such a cover out of fiberglass. Once in place over a 1958 T-bird convertible's rear passenger compartment, this cover restored at least some of the look, feel and pizzazz of the early 'Bird. Booth reportedly applied for a patent on his design and presented it to Ford officials, but apparently nothing ever came of it—nothing that benefited Bill Booth personally, that is.

With the groundwork already laid, it did not take long for Dearborn's design crew to come up with a better idea of their own. Credited primarily to stylist Bud Kaufman, Ford's fiberglass tonneau cover featured twin headrests and fitted almost like a glove while at the same time allowing the convertible top to operate unhindered. A pair of exclusive fender badges, a dash-mounted grab bar and four dazzling Kelsey-Hayes wire wheels completed the package. Presto! Instant Sports Roadster.

Quite expensive and clearly limited in everyday use (although that somewhat heavy cover could come off to free up more seating area), the two-seat Sports Roadster quickly encountered the same market realities faced by the first-generation Thunderbird. Sales never did amount to much, and thus the car was dropped after 1963. A similar dealer-installed package was offered in 1964 to convert the next restyled Thunderbird into a "Sports Roadster." But for the most part it would be nearly another 40 years before "two-seater" and "T-bird" would be used together in a sentence again.

SPECIFICATIONS

Engine: *300-horsepower 390 cubic-inch OHV V8, standard 340-horsepower 390 cubic-inch V8 with triple carburetors optional*

Bore & stroke: *4.05 x 3.78 inches*

Transmission: *Cruise-O-Matic automatic*

Suspension: *A-arms with coil springs in front; longitudinal leaf springs with solid axle in back*

Steering: *power-assisted re-circulating ball*

Brakes: *four-wheel hydraulic drums*

Price: *$5,439 in 1962, $5,563 in 1963*

Wheelbase: *113 inches*

Length: *205 inches*

Weight: *4,471 pounds in 1962; 4,395 pounds in 1963*

Model availability: *two-door, two-seat convertible (backseat remained in place topped by a fiberglass tonneau cover)*

Construction: *unitized body/frame*

Production: *1,427 in 1962; 455 in 1963*

1962-67 Shelby Cobra

Early in his career, Carroll Shelby's accomplishments as a driver was breaking land speed records at Bonneville in 1954 for Austin Healey and winning the 24-hours of Le Mans in 1959. Problems with his health in 1960 then forced him to give up driving, and he stepped out of the driver's seat to turn his attention to design. He had a vision for the automobile industry and went for it. And that vision has had a tremendous impact on the sports car world, with one of the greatest impacts being the development of the Cobra.

To say that Shelby's little Cobras were hot cars is a massive understatement. What else could have resulted after Shelby shoehorned a brutish American V8 beneath the aluminum bonnet of a spritely British sportster?

The original foundations for this hot little car was Britain's AC Ace, a truly tiny two-seat roadster. The V8 was Ford's "thinwall-cast" Windsor small-block, which displaced 221 cubic inches in base form. The Windsor V8 that Shelby began bolting into modified AC roadsters in February 1962 was the larger 260 cubic-inch

variety, an engine that made the new AC Cobra "one of the most impressive production sports cars we've ever driven," according to *Sports Car Graphic*.

The Shelby American shop in California produced only 75 260 Cobras before Ford Motor Company officials, midway though 1963, sent the word west that Ford would not be delivering any more 260 V8s. That was the bad news. The good news was that Ford would be replacing it with the new, larger 289 cubic-inch Windsor V8, which promised even more brute force from the Anglo-American hybrid. According to *Car Life*, the upgraded 289 Cobra could run from rest to 60 mph in only 5.7 seconds on the way to a top end of 133 mph. Other curbside kibitzers claimed performance much more extreme than that.

Those extremes then went well beyond anything known before in America after yet another engine swap, this time involving Ford's 427 cubic-inch "Le Mans" big-block V8.

Experiments in late 1964 led to the production of the ferocious 427 Cobra, built first in competition-only form beginning in October 1964. "Street-legal" models soon followed close behind. The total production for the 427 Cobra reached 348 before the madness stopped in 1967. Some of these street cars were fitted with less-powerful 428 Police Interceptor V8s to cut costs.

Dropping big-block power into the tightly confined aluminum body required numerous changes. A much stronger tubular frame was used and the antiquated transverse leaf springs appearing at both ends of the 260/289 Cobra were deleted in favor of coil springs at all four corners. Huge Girling four-wheel disc brakes were also installed, and the track was increased in the front and back.

To compensate for the wide track and to house a set of super-wide racing wheels and tires, the Cobra shell sprouted large fender flares and seven more inches of overall width. Its low, wide stance was also

accentuated by a longer, more aggressive nose formed with an enlarged snout for improved engine cooling.

Nothing else looked like a 427 Cobra, and nothing else surely ran like it. Reportedly all that power, coupled with all that rubber and those Girling discs made it possible to scream from 0 to 100 mph and back down to 0 again in only 13.8 seconds. That was not fast, that was big-time fast.

SPECIFICATIONS

Engine: 260 cubic-inch V8 in 1962-63
289 cubic-inch V8 in 1963-64
427 cubic-inch V8 in 1964-67 (some 428 V8s were also installed)

Transmission: four-speed manual

Brakes: hydraulic four-wheel Girling discs; 12-inch rotors in front, 11-inch rotors in back for 260 Cobra

Steering: worm and sector for 260 Cobra; rack and pinion for 289 and 427 Cobras

Price: $5,995 for base 260 Cobra & 289 Cobra; $7,495 for base 427 Cobra

Wheelbase: 90 inches

Width: 61 inches for 260 & 289 Cobras; 68 inches for 427 Cobra

Weight: 2,120 pounds for 260 Cobra; 2,170 pounds for 289 Cobra; 2,530 pounds for 427 Cobra

Model availability: two-door roadster

Construction: aluminum body on frame (specially fabricated tube frame used for big-block S/C Cobra)

Performance: 0-60 in 4.2 seconds; quarter-mile in 13.8 for 260 Cobra (Road & Track) 0-60 in 5.8 seconds for 289 Cobra (Car Life) 0-100-0 in 13.8 seconds for the 427 Cobra

Production: 75 260 Cobras, 580 289 Cobras, 348 427 Cobras

1964-¹/₂ Mustang

Lee Iacocca, Donald Frey and the rest knew they had themselves a hot seller even before the first Mustangs started kicking up dust on April 17, 1964. Initial forecasts claimed about 100,000 ponycars would be sold that first year, but Iacocca was far more optimistic. He had greater goals in mind, specifically Detroit's record for new model first-year sales, set by Ford's own Falcon four years before. Iacocca's battle cry became "417 by 4-17"—the plan was to sell at least 417,000 Mustangs by 4-17-65. No problem. By April 17, 1965, the tally read 418,812, amounting to 1,638 more Mustangs in 1965 than Falcons in 1960.

Of that record-breaking total, 121,538 were so-called "1964-1/2" models. Introduced in the middle of a model year, the first Mustang experienced an extended 18-month run that typically ended in August 1965. Most sources initially identified Ford's original ponycar as a "1965" model. But various running changes differentiated the cars built before August 1964 from those built afterwards, thus making it relatively easy to group the Mustang's first production run into 1964-1/2 and true 1965 categories. Identifying the differences is not possible in 25 words or less, so you will have to settle for the most recognizable clue: 1964-1/2 Mustangs used generators, 1965s used alternators. Production for the "true" 12-month 1965 model run was 559,451.

The first Mustang represented various different things to different drivers. According to *Car Life*, "it is a sports car, a gran turismo car, an economy car, a personal car, a rally car, a sprint car, a race car, a suburban car, and even a luxury car." Practicality and affordability were there in spades in base six-cylinder form, but also present was a sporty flair all its own. Bucket seats were standard inside, and that unforgettable body with its long hood and short rear deck helped even those in the know to forget that Iacocca's little baby was basically a made-over Falcon beneath that pretty skin. A long list of options including a console, a four-speed transmission and

V8 power enhanced the fun factor even further.

Really big news came in June 1964 when the 271-horsepower High Performance 289 V8 joined that list. And even more sportiness arrived in September as a third bodystyle, the 2+2 fastback, joined the original coupe and convertible. Designed by Gail Halderman, the 2+2 featured a trendy sweeping roofline and a rear seat that folded down to open up a large, flat cargo floor extending from the trunk into the passenger compartment.

The Mustang's official press introduction came on Monday, April 13, at the New York World's Fair. After listening to Iacocca speak about the youth-oriented market, the crowd was introduced to the

most anticipated automobile since the Model A replaced the Model T in 1928.

An unprecedented broadcast barrage then began on Thursday evening, April 16, as television commercials ran on all three networks at the same time. Countless print ads followed in essentially every major magazine and newspaper that weekend. But who had time to pick up a paper? Starting on Friday, much of America was busy flocking into the nearest Ford showroom to at least see the car they would be reading about soon enough.

Buying one was not so easy. The few Mustangs on hand were immediately snapped up and 22,000 additional orders were placed that first day. A two-month wait for delivery was common, and many dealerships reportedly locked their doors and called police when the rush grew too great. It was estimated that four million people pushed their way into showrooms that first weekend.

And the pace did not slow down. Midway through the 1966 run the Mustang broke yet another sales record previously held by the Falcon. Just before noon on Wednesday, February 23, the one millionth Mustang rolled off the assembly line, making it the quickest to reach seven digits. Some 35 years later Mustang lovers are still flocking into dealerships to buy the compact that started the ponycar craze, even as Chevrolet's Camaro and Pontiac's Firebird have become museum pieces.

SPECIFICATIONS

Engine: 170 cubic-inch six-cylinder, standard

260 cubic-inch Windsor small-block V8, optional; 289 cubic-inch Windsor small-block V8, optional

Transmission: three-speed manual, standard; four-speed manual and automatic were optional

Brakes: four-wheel hydraulic drums (front discs were optional)

Suspension: short/long control arms with coil springs in front, longitudinal leaf springs and solid axle in back

Price: $2,368 (with base six-cylinder)

Wheelbase: 108 inches

Length: 181.6 inches

Weight: 2,449 pounds (with base six-cylinder)

Model availability: two-door coupe and two-door convertible

Construction: unitized body/frame stamped in steel

Production: 121,538

1966 GT40 MK II

It remains an unforgettable photo: three Ford-powered racers rumbling in the rain across the finish line in France as the checkered flag waved. It was Sunday, June 19, 1966. After waiting roughly three years and 24 hours, Henry Ford II had finally bested Enzo Ferrari where it counted most—LeMans. And along with embarrassing his Italian antagonist, Henry II also became the first American automaker to bring Les Vingt-Quatre Heures laurels back home to the States.

It had taken a few years to get things together, but the GT40 was finally the king of the racing world in 1966. And it remained so until 1969. Four straight GT40 wins at LeMans helped salt away Ford's image as the "Total Performance" company

Enzo Ferrari deserves a fair share of the credit for the creation of the car that eventually overshadowed his prancing horses in the international endurance racing arena. Ferrari had approached Ford in early 1963 with a proposition: for $18 million, he would merge his exotic car company with Henry Ford II's. The match looked good for both sides. Enzo would get

the financial stability he sought and Henry II would overnight find himself with a world-class sports car.

But it was not to be. Ford's high-pressure negotiation tactics intimidated Ferrari, and he quickly changed his mind, rejecting Dearborn's $10 million counter offer in May 1963. A furious Henry Ford II then immediately demanded revenge. "If you can't join 'em, beat 'em."

Less then two months later, Lee Iacocca contacted British sports/racer builder Eric Broadley, the man behind the innovative Lola GT, a mid-engine machine based on a monocoque chassis. Broadley then teamed up with Ford engineer Roy Lunn for the second time—the two had worked together on the mid-engine Mustang I concept car in 1962—to build a Lola-like Ferrari-beater for Henry II. The team needed only 10 months to have a

prototype ready for LeMans trials in April 1964. The name for the car, GT40, was in reference to the low-slung vehicle's height—a mere 40 inches.

Later designated "Mark I," the original GT40 coupe was based on a mid-engine monocoque foundation formed mostly of folded sheet steel. The nose and tail, which both tilted open, were made of fiberglass, as were the aircraft-style doors that cut into the roof. Power was initially supplied by Ford's exotic 256-cid Indianapolis V8, but this troublesome all-aluminum small-block was soon traded for a more reliable production-based 289 V8 with iron block and heads.

Teething problems kept the GT40 from taking a checkered flag in 1964, after which time Carroll Shelby was given the task of making the car into a winner. Things then really got cooking that year after the introduction of the revamped Mk II, the car

that gave Henry II his revenge over Enzo at LeMans one year later.

More aggressive-looking bodywork front and rear only represented icing on the cake for the mean and nasty 200-mph Mk II. In place of the Mk I's small-block came Ford's NASCAR-dominating 7-liter big-block, the famed FE-series 427 V8. Output was a whopping 485 horsepower.

It was its steadfast durability, coupled with all that power, that made the Mk II so dominant at LeMans in 1966. An even lighter, more powerful Mk IV variant then won again in 1967 before jealous rules-makers banned the 7-liter GT40. No problem. The small-block Mk I returned to LeMans in 1968 and made it three in a row for the GT40. That very same Mk I, chassis number 1075, won again in 1969 in the closest finish ever after 24 hours of racing in France.

In 1970 Ford shut down its mighty racing operation, but least the Blue Oval went out with a bang.

SPECIFICATIONS

Engine: 427 cubic-inch OHV V8 with aluminum heads

Horsepower: 485 at 6,200 rpm

Compression: 10.5:1

Bore and Stroke: 4.24 x 3.78 inches

Fuel delivery: single 780-cfm Holley four-barrel carburetor

Transmission: Ford-built T-44 four-speed transaxle

Wheelbase: 95 inches

Weight: 2,700 pounds

Production: 133 total chassis built for GT40 family Two Mk II prototypes and eight Mk II production models were built Three more lightweight Alan Mann Mk II GT40s were also

1969 Mercury Cyclone Spoiler II

Robert McNamara may have agreed to the AMA anti-racing "ban" in 1957, but it was not long before Fords were back on the track in force with full factory support. By 1963, the big 427 Galaxies were winning regularly, and Mercury's 427-powered Marauders were no slouches either. Speeding past 150 mph was no problem for these boulevard brutes, and the top end on NASCAR super-speedways kept climbing from there.

Then came the wall. Physical laws being constant, maximum big-block horsepower could only do so much with a stock body that possessed all the aerodynamics of a brick. The limit was about 175 mph as all those horses simply could not beat the wind.

Although Ford and Mercury drivers managed to slip through this barrier to some degree in 1968 with relatively sleek Fairlane and Cyclone fastback bodies, their slight advantage was soon lost as Dodge countered with

its new Charger 500, named after NASCAR's minimum production requirement. To take a special model racing on stock car tracks, an automaker had to build at least 500 regular-production examples of that car for sale to the public.

Special features on Dodge's limited-production 1969 Charger 500 included its flush-mounted grille and rear window, modifications that reduced aerodynamic drag considerably. This, in turn, resulted in higher speeds at the racetrack, even higher than FoMoCo's new fastbacks.

Dearborn then quickly countered. As the Dodge boys were showing off their new "aero-racer" in Charlotte late in 1968, Ford's racing chief, Jacque Passino, was heading across town to Holman-Moody, where

Ralph Moody had already built a similar machine based on the fastback Fairlane. Using longer Cyclone fenders from Mercury, Moody had fashioned an extended nose that could slice through the wind with ease and supply ample downforce to help keep the tires on the track. Passino took Moody's prototype back to Michigan for Bunkie Knudsen's approval, which was surely a given. Ford's NASCAR coordinator, Charlie Gray, then suggested that the new model be named after the super-speedway then being built in Alabama near the town of Talladega.

To meet NASCAR's production requirement, officials at Ford's Atlanta plant dedicated most of the January 1969 assembly schedule run to the new 1969 Talladega. The Fairlane-based Talladega featured special fenders with stamped steel extensions welded on, a flush-mounted Fairlane Cobra grille and a unique downward-sloping header panel that filled the space between the grille and hood. Additional modifications included rocker panels that were cut and re-rolled one inch higher than stock sheetmetal,

an expensive trick that allowed race teams to lower Talladega bodies that extra inch over their racing frames while still maintaining NASCAR's rigidly enforced minimum ground clearance.

Mercury also manufactured a kissin'-cousin to the Talladega in 1969, the Cyclone Spoiler Sports Special, or Cyclone Spoiler II. Looking quite similar with its long, dropped snout and rolled rocker panels, the Spoiler II in fact differed much in detail, only because the Cyclone and Fairlane bodies themselves were not identical. Spoiler IIs also featured a less formidable 351 cubic-inch small-block V8 as standard equipment. Ford fitted all Talladega with the 428 Cobra Jet big-block. At least Mercury's Cyclone Spoiler II was flashier, thanks to a rear wing, more prominent striping and contrasting roof paint.

Once legally racing, Mercury's Spoiler II was overshadowed by its Ford running mate and Dodge's modified Chargers. Talladega drivers scored 26 wins and Charger 500s took 18 checkered flags in 1969. The Mercury Cyclone Spoiler II wins numbered only four that year.

SPECIFICATIONS

Engine: 290-horsepower 351 cubic-inch Windsor small-block V8

Bore & stroke: 4.00 x 3.50 inches

Compression: 10.7:1

Fuel delivery: single four-barrel carburetor

Transmission: Select-Shift automatic

Wheelbase: 116 inches

Height: 52.6 inches

Model availability: two-door fastback dressed up in either blue-accented "Dan Gurney Special" or red-accented "Cale Yarborough Special" adornments

Construction: body on frame (with various body modifications to improve aerodynamics)

Production: 353 known today

1969-70 Boss Mustang

When Bunkie Knudsen arrived in Dearborn in February 1968 he brought along some strong beliefs concerning the Mustang. In his words, the popular ponycar was "a good-looking automobile, but there are a tremendous number of people out there who want good-looking automobiles with performance. If a car looks like it's going fast and doesn't go fast, people get turned off."

Such was the case for the first big-block Mustang, introduced for 1967. A relative weakling compared to Chevy's truly hot SS 396 Camaro, the 390 Mustang was then upstaged in April 1968 by the 428 Cobra Jet model, a super-strong horse that instantly put Dearborn on the musclecar map. But why stop there?

Chevrolet also had the Z/28 Camaro, then the best of its breed. Created with SCCA Trans-Am road racing in mind, this hot little honey could handle and stop as well as it could accelerate. Big-block ponycars were quicker, but they did not deal with the curves well with all that extra weight up front.

More than one GM genius also jumped over to Ford at Knudsen's invitation, and they brought more than one GM idea along with them. Among these people was designer Larry Shinoda, the man who had drawn up the Z/28's sporty image in 1967. Hired in May 1968, Shinoda was presented with the task of besting a performance legend he had helped create.

Shinoda contributed the new car's stripes, spoilers and window slats, as well as its name.

Two Boss Mustangs were born in 1969, both originally developed concurrently by Ford's performance contractor, Kar Kraft Engineering, in Brighton, Michigan. Kar Kraft began building prototypes in August 1968 after Knudsen demanded that his engineers produce "absolutely the best-handling street car available on the American market." The Boss 302 Mustang was the

result. The other Mustang, the beastly Boss 429, was a big-block boulevard brute best suited for straight-line speed runs.

The Kar Kraft crew, lead by Roy Lunn, developed and built the Boss 429, while Ford Engineering took over the Boss 302 project after prototype work was completed. Engineer Matt Donner was the man responsible for the excellent Boss 302 chassis, which quickly impressed critics with the way it hugged the road.

How did the Boss 302 stack up to Chevy's hot-handling Z/28? "In showroom trim, car for car, the Mustang was close, but I can't really say [it] was superior," added Shinoda. On the track, the battle between the two arch-rivals was a toss-up.

Chevrolet's Trans-Am Camaro took home SCCA racing laurels in 1969, while Ford's Boss 302 put the Mustang back on top in 1970. As for street performance, both machines relied on specially built 290-horsepower 302 cubic-inch small-block V8s.

Ford's first Boss 302 rolled off the line on April 17, 1969, and the breed continued on into 1970 before falling victim to Henry Ford II's complete attitude reversal concerning his company's racing involvement. And like its 302 cousin, the Boss 429 Mustang was also rapidly developed in late 1968, then quickly cancelled early in 1970.

The Boss 429 was built solely to legalize its 375-horsepower "semi-hemi" V8 for NASCAR racing. NASCAR's production standard did not specify the vehicle, just the engine. As long as Ford brought at least 500 Boss 429 V8s to the dance, it did not matter how they were dressed. On the street, the Boss satisfied demands beneath a Mustang hood. On NASCAR tracks, it then threw its weight around behind the extended snout of Ford's Talladega.

The Boss 429 Mustang hit the streets in January 1969, nearly three months ahead of the Boss 302. Development of the Boss 429 V8 dated back to 1968 after Ford had introduced its 385-series "thin-wall" big-block family for its luxury lines. Engineers immediately began plotting a way to take this new engine racing. To do this, they cast a special reinforced cylinder block, on top of that went exotic iron heads with sewer-sized ports, massive inclined valves and hemispherical combustion chambers. By the time this engine reached production, those iron heads were traded for weight-saving aluminum units with revised combustion chambers. These chambers were not quite hemispherical, thus the "semi-hemi" designation.

Whatever the name, the big Boss 429 did not drop easily into the ponycar platform, thus the reason behind Kar Kraft's continued involvement. Various labor-intensive modifications were required, including widening the engine compartment by two inches, and these changes were best made on a small, specialized assembly line. Once shoehorned between Mustang flanks, Ford's semi-hemi too turned a few heads.

SPECIFICATIONS

Engine: 290-horsepower 302 cubic-inch Cleveland-head small-block V8
375-horsepower 429 cubic-inch aluminum-head big-block V8

Transmission: four-speed manual (automatic not available)

Steering: re-circulating ball

Wheels & tires: 15x7 stamped steel rims with F60x15 Wide-Oval tires, Boss 302 (Magnum 500 five-spoke wheels optional)
15x7 Magnum 500 wheels with F60x15 Wide-Oval tires, Boss 429

Brakes: four-wheel hydraulic with front discs, rear drums

Suspension: both used short/long-arms and coil springs up front, longitudinal leaf springs and a solid axle in back; both featured heavy-duty anti-sway bars, springs and shock absorbers, with the shocks in back "staggered" to help prevent axle windup; Boss 429 front suspension geometry changed to make room up front for larger engine

Wheelbase: 108 inches

Height: 50.4 inches

Weight: 3,250 pounds, Boss 302
3,530 pounds, Boss 429

Model availability: two-door "Sports Roof" fastback

Construction: unitized body/frame

Quarter-mile performance: 14.09 seconds at 102.85 mph (Boss 429, according to Car Life test)

Production: 1,628 in 1969, 7,013 in 1970 (Boss 302)
857 in 1969, 499 in 1970 (Boss 429)

1971-80: The Sun also Rises

BELOW: *The "Cobra-Jet" 429-cubic inch V8 had a bore and stroke of 4.36 x 3.59 inches and developed a massive 370 bhp. Recession, fuel crises and ever-tightening emissions legislation laid it to rest at the end of 1971.*

Lee Iacocca never did like what happened to his precious little ponycar in the late-Sixties, especially after Bunkie Knudsen took command at Ford. "As soon as Knudsen arrived, he began adding weight to the Mustang and making it bigger," wrote Iacocca in 1984. "Within a few years of its introduction, the Mustang was no longer a sleek horse, it was more like a fat pig. In 1968, Knudsen added a monster engine with double the horsepower. To support the engine, he had to widen the car. By 1971, the Mustang was no longer the same car." Nor was Semon Knudsen president of Ford Motor Company. As of December 1970, that job belonged to Iacocca.

At the time, Bunkie's beloved musclecar was fast fading from the scene, a victim of Washington's increasing pressure on Detroit to build cleaner-running engines and safer cars. But lowering emissions and heightening automotive safety required manufactures to spend more on development, and these additional costs were then passed onto customers. Buyers then began looking elsewhere for more affordable transportation, with most turning their attentions to Japan. Having first gained a meager foothold on the American market as the 1950s closed, Japanese imports had steadily gained popularity on this side of the Pacific as the 1960s rolled on. Though few in Detroit paid any attention whatsoever to these Japanese imports early on, all had taken notice by the end of the decade.

"Failure to recognize the foreign threat before it was too late left all American automakers wondering what had hit them within a few short years."

Ford's first notable response to the Japanese import invasion had come along even before Bunkie was booted out. Introduced in April 1969, the affordable, compact Maverick was hailed as the "the first car of the Seventies at 1960s prices." Henry Ford II then followed that up by personally unveiling an even smaller car, the Pinto, in the spring of 1970. That opened the door for Iacocca, who used the Pinto platform as a base for his "little jewel," the downsized Mustang II, which rolled out to rave reviews late in 1973.

"The affordable, compact Maverick was hailed as the "the first car of the Seventies at 1960s prices." Henry Ford II then followed that up by personally unveiling an even smaller car, the Pinto... That opened the door for Iacocca, who used the Pinto platform as a base for his "little jewel," the downsized Mustang II, which rolled out to rave reviews late in 1973.

RIGHT: *The 1974 Mustang II had become a domesticated animal, now featuring a handy hatch-back, convenient for the groceries. Up front, the option of V8 power had been withdrawn.*

ABOVE: *The sumptuous interior of the 1971 Maverick LTD Show Car included a power sunroof and leather trim to the seats, doors and headlining.*

Mustang II madness at first rivaled the feeding frenzy that had followed the original Mustang's debut in April 1964 then tailed off considerably. But Iacocca's pint-sized ponycar was not alone in its fall, as downward trends became the order of the day around Detroit during the 1970s. Failure to recognize the foreign threat before it was too late left all American automakers wondering what had hit them within a few short years.

At Ford the decade began with much promise and even a little celebration—the latter coming in June 1971 when Dearborn honored the 75th anniversary of Henry Ford's first ride in his Quadricycle. Net corporate income hit a record high the following year, and Ford Division once again finished just a hair behind Chevrolet in the annual sales race. Then the bottom fell out overnight.

Ford Motor Company's market share for 1973 dropped to its lowest point since 1952, and corporate earnings declined by 58 per cent in 1974. A short-lived turnaround did come in 1978, spiked by Ford's greatest sales month ever in June. But another downturn quickly followed, leading to the corporation's worst market share score (20.29 per cent) of the postwar era. In 1980 Ford suffered its greatest losses ever, $1.54 million dollars, and that year Chevrolet built nearly twice as many cars compared to its old rival.

RIGHT: The King Cobra was equipped with extremely handsome, lightweight, all-alloy wheels that featured a neat, wire-spoke effect design.

Various factors contributed to this downfall, not the least of which was 1973-74's "gas crunch," fueled by the Arab oil embargo. Skyrocketing gasoline prices instantly convinced Americans to start shopping for small, efficient automobiles, like those wearing Datsun and Toyoda nameplates. Prior to 1970 the import share of the U.S. market had hovered around 10 per cent. It was 15 per cent within a few years and nearly 23 per cent by 1979.

A second, slightly less alarming energy crisis, this one spurred on by the Iranian revolution, occurred in 1980 to help wring out more red ink. Throw in America's growing "stagflation"—the new term for the combination of stagnant economy and double-digit inflation then hindering the market—and 1980 could not have been a worse time to be in the car-building business. Not since the early 1930s had things looked so bleak. Of course all of Detroit experienced the same stresses during the 1970s, but Ford's troubles were compounded further by headline-making lawsuits involving faulty transmissions (that shifted into gear by themselves) and exploding gas tanks (located poorly in the Pinto platform).

"Various factors contributed to Ford's downfall, not the least of which was 1973-74's "gas crunch," fueled by the Arab oil embargo. Skyrocketing gasoline prices instantly convinced Americans to start shopping for small, efficient automobiles, like those wearing Datsun and Toyota nameplates.

ABOVE: *The hood decal on this 1978 King Cobra is big and brash but maximum output was by now quoted at 139 bhp, which did not sound quite so impressive.*

Federal lawmakers did not make things any easier by mandating a counter-attack to the rising import menace using their Corporate Average Fuel Economy standards. Announced in 1975 as part of the Energy Policy and Conservation Act, the CAFE system required each automaker to meet a minimum average miles-per-gallon count for all its cars beginning in 1978. The CAFE baseline that first year was 18 mpg, but it would not remain at that level—by 1985, the bar was raised to 27.5 mpg.

Though forcing American manufacturers to start thinking more efficiently did eventually pay off, Washington at first only aided the enemy as CAFE-inspired higher development costs continued to hike domestic car prices across the board. Foreign imports then became even more enticing, leaving demand for those big American "gas hogs" down in the dumps.

Like its rivals, Ford responded by downsizing yet again, this time with its bigger cars. First came a "luxury compact" Granada, in 1975, followed by the new Fox-chassis Fairmont in 1978. Even the Thunderbird—which had grown to enormous proportions by 1976—went under the axe, first in 1977, and again in 1980.

Getting the axe as well was Lido Anthony Iacocca. Like his predecessor, Bunkie Knudsen, Iacocca had grown to big for his britches, at least as far as Henry Ford II was concerned. And like Bunkie, he was given an unceremonious boot to those britches, this one coming less than a month after Ford's big 75th birthday party in June 1978. After 32 years in Dearborn, Iacocca was released, in Henry II's publicly stated words, "for insubordination." Privately, the big boss plain and simply had grown to dislike the aggressive marketing genius, who was then only 54 and still as much a prime mover as he was back in 1964.

The man who invented the ponycar was not out of work for long. In November 1978 he joined Chrysler Corporation and proceeded to work wonders there with a long-standing company on the verge of oblivion. Among Chrysler's early saviors were its all-new minivans, Dodge Caravan and Plymouth Voyager, introduced in 1984. Not coincidentally, these two "garagable" vans looked an awful lot like a concept (named Carousel) developed at Ford during the early 1970s, an idea that stood ready in 1973 to go into production two years later had not an energy crisis emerged to kill it before it was born.

Apparently Lee Iacocca had taken more than his Rolodex while packing up his Dearborn office.

1971 Ford Pinto

ord had tried to think small during the 1960s, but the effort somehow managed to morph into something more. More size. More money. More features. Dearborn's first small car, the Falcon, had debuted in 1960 to help turn back the import invasion, which was then led by Germany's Volkswagen. Affordable and practical, the Falcon set sales records at first then dwindled off as it grew in size and cost. Ford's piece of the compact-car pie in 1962 had been 36 per cent, it was a mere 8 per cent by 1970.

By that time the once-popular Falcon was an easily overlooked mid-sized offering on its last legs standing by while foreign compacts continued gaining ground. Import sales made up 15 per cent of the total U.S. market in 1970, and Japanese cars were just getting warmed up. Although Ford's latest compact, the Maverick, had taken off like a rocket in April 1969, it still was not able to stem the growing import tide.

"The fact remains Maverick did not make a big dent in VW, they continued along their merry way," said Ford Motor Company vice president and Ford Division general manager John Naughton in a September 1970 Motor Trend interview. "Maverick had been successful and had attracted an enormous amount of people, but head to head with VW, we weren't taking them on like we had hoped to. We knew we had to have a smaller car."

Indeed, the Maverick was not really a small car, not by international standards. Nor was the original Falcon. But that did not necessarily mean Ford did not know how to compete with the Europeans. "We have built small cars on a worldwide basis for years and years, but the company had never built a true sub-compact type car in this country," added Naughton.

Then along came the Pinto, an attractive little pony that galloped along on a 94-inch wheelbase, a half-inch less than the VW Beetle's. Called "the second part of a 1-2 punch against the imports" by Ford people, the Pinto appeared in September 1970, about the same time Chevrolet rolled out its own pint-sized Bug-fighter, Vega.

According to *Road & Track*, the slightly larger, more refined Vega was "by far the more interesting design." Yet Ford's sub-compact still won out in a head-to-head battle. "Pinto happened to be the more pleasant car to drive in everyday use and carries a price tag some $172 less," continued the *R&T* review. "To be sure, there is 'less car' in the Pinto. But thanks to a smoother engine, a superior gearbox, somewhat greater comfort for the driver and better finish throughout, it is subjectively the nicer car." Chevy sold nearly 275,000

Vegas for 1971, while Pinto sales that first year topped 352,000, followed by another 480,000 in 1972.

Shared by Lincoln-Mercury's newly imported Capri, that "smoother engine" came from British Ford's Cortina, which ceased coming across the Atlantic to America once the Pinto arrived. Displacing only 1.6 liters, this overhead-valve four-cylinder produced a meager 75 horsepower, compared to 90 horses for the Vega's 2.3-liter four. Though this power shortage did not prevent the Pinto from outselling its GM rival, Ford engineers still added an optional six-cylinder in 1975.

Other than that, few additions were entered into Dearborn's sub-compact equation during a successful 10-year run, and that had been the plan from the beginning. "The Model T lasted virtually unchanged for 19 years, and that in mind I felt we should try to accomplish the same objective with the Pinto," said Henry Ford II while introducing his new compact to the press in the spring of 1970. "Any changes in the Pinto will be aimed at making it a better car and not just different looking."

Engineers, of course, did have to address a potentially fatal fuel tank design problem that landed Ford in court and briefly transformed the

SPECIFICATIONS

Engine: 75-horsepower 1.6 liter OHV four-cylinder

Bore & stroke: 3.19 x 3.08 inches

Compression: 8.4:1

Fuel delivery: two-barrel carburetor

Transmission: four-speed manual, standard; three-speed automatic, optional

Steering: rack and pinion

Brakes: hydraulic four-wheel drums

Suspension: independent control arms with coil springs in front; longitudinal leaf springs and solid axle (with staggered shock absorbers) in back

Price: $1,919

Wheelbase: 94 inches

Length: 163 inches

Weight: 1,949 pounds

Model availability: two-door sedan, joined by a three-door Runabout later in the year

Construction: unitized body/frame

Production: 352,402, both models.

Pinto into the latest star of Johnny Carson's "Tonight Show" dialogue. Such slings and arrows aside, the Pinto still helped keep Dearborn competitive during tough times and did so for 10 successful years before another new compact, Escort, came along in 1981.

1971 Mercury Capri

ord Division was not alone in the quest to "think small," as Motor Trend called Henry Ford II's new strategy for the 1970s. Upscale Mercury too typically followed in Ford's tracks, just as it had done in 1960 when it introduced its first compact, Comet. A relatively affordable machine that existed a few steps up in prestige above the Falcon, this stylish small car was joined in 1967 by Cougar, a more luxurious variation on Ford's ponycar theme. As with their

entirely new compact all of its own that year, a sporty two-door coupe that borrowed a name first familiarized on Lincoln models in 1952: Capri.

counterparts from Fords, these two Mercurys then grew in size as the 1970s arrived, bringing with them economic pressures that forced Lincoln-Mercury officials to also rethink their definition of "compact." This resulted in an all-new Comet for 1971, again a knock-off of a Ford product, in this case Maverick. But the L-M Division also had an

Already a sensation overseas, the latest, greatest Capri had first appeared in London in December 1968 and was quickly nicknamed the "European Mustang." Its sharp styling was even sexier than the first ponycar's. And its standard bucket seats, front disc brakes and four-speed stick all worked in concert to impress

buyers in Great Britain and West Germany with an all-new form of affordable transport, one that was every bit as fun as it was practical. By December 1969, Capri sales had hit 70,000 in the U.K., 115,000 in Germany.

Though commonly called a German-built product, the Capri was actually assembled by Ford in the European plants in Great Britain and Belgium, along with West Germany. Emissions-legal Capri coupes imported to America were introduced in L-M dealerships on April 17, 1970—the Mustang's 5th birthday. On U.S. soil these first cars were identified both as 1971 models and "Mercury Capris" even

though they did not wear Mercury badges. Calendar-year 1970 sales for the 1971 Capri amounted to 17,300, a new record for a first-year import in America.

Motor Trend's staffers were so impressed, they named the new Capri their first "Import Car of the Year" in 1970, and *Road Test* magazine bestowed a similar honor in 1971. "If any modern automotive product ever reaches the universality of the Model T, it will be the Capri," claimed *Petersen's Import Buyer's Guide 1971*.

About 1.17 million Capri coupes, with both four- and six-cylinder power, were built by 1974, followed by another 404,000 Capri II models from 1975 to 1977. An even smaller Capri, this one a two-door roadster, appeared later in 1991.

SPECIFICATIONS

Engine: 71-horsepower 1600cc (97.6 cubic inches) OHV four-cylinder

Bore & stroke: 3.19 x 3.08 inches

Compression: 8.0:1

Fuel delivery: single two-barrel carburetor

Transmission: four-speed manual transmission

Steering: rack and pinion

Brakes: power-assisted hydraulic with front discs, rear drums

Suspension: MacPherson struts with coil springs in front; longitudinal leaf springs and solid axle (with staggered shock absorbers) in back

Price: $2,295

Wheelbase: 100.8 inches

Length: 167.8 inches

Height: 52 inches

Weight: 2,135 pounds

Model availability: four-passenger two-door sport coupe

Construction: unitized body/frame

Production: 17,300 during calendar year 1970

1974 Mustang II

Lee Iacocca never did like the way his baby began growing up after 1966. A bigger Mustang was by no means a better Mustang in his humble opinion, and this belief was forged long before an even larger ponycar came along in 1971. By that time Iacocca was not the only one upset. Loyal Mustang buyers too were letting their feelings known through the mail. No longer a sporty compact, it was more of a "luxury bus" as one protesting letter-writer put it.

As early as November 1969, Iacocca had been suggesting a new direction for the Mustang, one that would bring it back closer to his original ideal. Success of the new, compact Maverick in 1970 did not hurt his cause in the least, and the groundwork was quickly laid for a redesigned, downsized Mustang.

Italy's famed design studio, Ghia, was responsible for creating the first prototype. Ford had bought a controlling interest in the Turin firm in November 1970, and within a few months Ghia head Alejandro de Tomaso had turned out a sleek little machine that started the Mustang II project rolling. Iacocca's "little jewel" was then officially introduced on August 28, 1973.

Measuring but 96.2 inches from hub to hub, down 13 inches from the really big 1973 Mustang, the Mustang II was also four inches skinnier, 14 inches shorter, and some 300 pounds lighter. New design features included rack-and-pinion steering, exceptional noise and vibration reduction, and a frugal 2.3-liter four-cylinder engine. A 2.8-liter V6 was optional for the four models offered: the base Mustang II coupe, a three-door fastback, an upscale Ghia, and the familiar Mach 1.

Proving that less sometimes is more, the truly small Mustang II set a sales pace nearly as quick as its ancestor had 10 years before. The

Arab oil embargo undoubtedly had something to do with the mad rush that developed in the fall of 1973 as many Americans became convinced that small, economical cars represented the only way to fly into the future. More than 385,000 buyers took flight behind the wheels of Mustang IIs in 1974, a good number of those perhaps jumping on the bandwagon after *Motor Trend* named Ford's slimmed-down ponycar its "Car of the Year" in January 1974. In *Motor Trend*'s words, this new breed stood as "a total departure from the fat old horse of the recent past."

Others were not so quick to praise the reborn Mustang. "While the Mach 1's general concept is enthusiast-oriented," claimed *Car and Driver*, "its poor acceleration, wide-ratio transmission and overweight chassis leave too much of its

undeniably sporting flavor unsupported by nourishment." *Car Craft* called the car "regrettably underpowered," then predicted that Ford would probably have to offer a V8 version, and soon.

An optional V8 did arrive in 1975, but sales that year still fell by more than 50 per cent as the attraction quickly faded. Among other things, many buyers had already grown dissatisfied with the car's cramped quarters. And it seemed soaring gas prices could only compromise a Mustang buyers standards so far, a fact demonstrated in 1977 when sales dropped down to the 150,000 plateau, a place not all that much higher than the disappointing levels achieved in 1971-73. Those sagging sales then signaled the need for yet another redesigned Mustang.

While work progressed on this project, Ford made one last stab at pumping up the Mustang II image in 1978. Built for five months, the 1978 King Cobra was yet another striped, spoilered,

and spatted excuse for a performance car. "With the real muscle-car era now no more than memory," wrote *Car Craft*'s John Asher, "cars like the Ford King Cobra are becoming the machismo machines of the late Seventies."

And that was not a good thing. Fortunately another all-new Mustang arrived in 1979 to save the day.

1975 Ford Granada

Many Americans still were not all that fond of really small, plainly simple cars in the early 1970s, which helps to partially explain why a not-so-small small car like Maverick did so well initially and continued doing even better while growing in price and presence. Plans were even in place to take the Maverick up to an even higher level for 1975. The thinking was to let the Pinto stave off the cheap imports, while Ford felt that it was time for the rest of the motor company to get back to building better cars again.

Then came an oil embargo and an energy crisis, joined just in time by a serious economic recession. Suddenly affordable, efficient compacts became even more important than ever before, resulting in the Maverick staying on board in its original form.

In truth, product planners in Dearborn probably got greedy, even amidst tough economic conditions. The original Maverick was still selling quite well, so why fix it if it was not broken? At the same time, why not just add another model line to take advantage of those Americans who did not like to think small but still could not imagine spending their hard-earned cash on something much bigger. In 1975 Ford offered the Granada to this new market group, called the "car designed for the times" by promotional people.

Though it was based on the existing four-door Maverick platform, the Granada (along with its new Monarch running mate from Mercury) was a little wider, considerably longer and much heavier than Ford's first compact for the 1970s. It was still classed as a compact, but uncharacteristically (for a

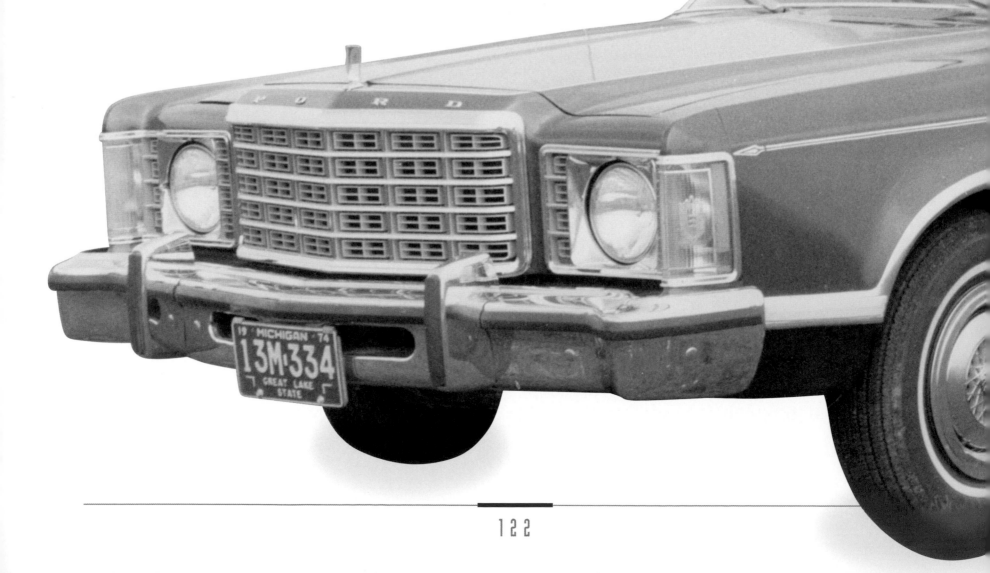

compact) the look and feel convinced customers that they were buying something more. Much more. Eugene Bordinat's stylists even copied much of the Granada's image from one of world's finest luxury automobiles, something television commercials openly admitted to—were you one of the many innocent bystanders in 1975 who reportedly mistook Ford's new "deluxe compact" for a Mercedes-Benz? Perhaps if you had squinted your eyes a bit...

"If we had expected a surrogate Mercedes, we'd be disappointed," said a *Road & Track* review. "But if we look at the moderate price tag and think of the Granada as a reasonable-size interpretation of the traditional American car with a little inspiration from Europe, there's no problem liking it."

Many Americans did, which was proved by the sales for 1975 when they surpassed 300,000, and this was for the car that *Motor Trend*'s John Christy called perhaps "the most important Ford since the first Mustang." Granada popularity remained relatively strong during a nice run that eventually ended in 1982.

SPECIFICATIONS

Engine: *250 cubic-inch OHV V8*

Bore & stroke: *3.68 x 3.91 inches*

Transmission: *three-speed manual; automatic optional*

Steering: *re-circulating ball, power steering optional*

Suspension: *independent A-arms with coil springs in front; longitudinal leaf springs and a solid axle in back*

Brakes: *hydraulic discs; power-assist optional*

Price: *ranged from $3,698 to $4,326*

Wheelbase: *109.9 inches*

Length: *198 inches, base model; 200 inches, Ghia*

Width: *74 inches*

Weight: *ranged from 3,230 to 3,423 pounds*

Model availability: *two- and four-door sedans offered in base and upscale Ghia forms*

Construction: *unitized body/frame with front subframe*

Production: *302,649*

1977 Ford Fiesta

Ford had started thinking small even before the so-called "Energy Crisis" began in 1973. Make that really small. Originally code-named "Bobcat," the truly tiny Fiesta was given the go-ahead in 1972 following several years of planning and development, although the target then obviously was the other side of the Atlantic, where itty-bitty affordable cars offering itty-bitty operating costs had been hot tickets for quite some time. By the late-1970s, the small-engine (less than 1200cc), small-car class then waiting for the Fiesta in Europe made up some 30 per cent of market.

The project's name change came once it was decided to offer this pint-sized compact—which by the way eventually emerged as Ford's first front-wheel-drive model—to American buyers, too. Mercury was already using the Bobcat badge in North America, so it simply became the natural choice to switch to the Fiesta label worldwide.

Ford introduced the German-built Fiesta in Europe first in the summer of 1976, with a U.S. debut coming later in 1977. According to Dearborn officials, the original idea was not necessarily to build a cheap budget buggy, but simply a more affordable, scaled-down version of their typical cars complete with a nice array of options and model choices. In Ford's words, these all-new small cars would first and foremost "reflect today's need for maximum efficiency and the growing importance of energy conservation."

Energy conservation was guaranteed by a little transverse-mounted four-cylinder powerplant that allowed the base Fiesta to squeeze about 30 miles out of a gallon of gas, even with the low-octane gas found in some European countries. But along with that, the first Fiesta offered buyers in Europe various far-from-mundane choices: slightly larger, more powerful engines and four different models topped by an upscale Ghia version. Imagine that; pure price-conscious practicality combined with a little peppy pizzazz—no wonder some sources in Europe considered the Fiesta to be, in *Motor Trend*'s words, "perhaps the most important automotive project in history." A bit of an overstatement, of course, but remember, these were almost desperate times when no one could predict how high gas prices would go and the future of fossil-fueled transport looked bleaker than ever.

Though things then did not look quite so dark in the West, no one was waiting to pooh-pooh the little front-driver when it appeared in American dealerships. While no engine options came with it in 1977, the first U.S.-marketed Fiesta did offer the various décor options, including the $725 Ghia package, which alone cost 20 per cent as much as a complete base model. Other optional frivolities, such as air conditioning and a flip-up sun roof, soon appeared to further defeat the Fiesta's budget-minded purposes.

Fiesta popularity in America remained healthy throughout its four-year run. Sales in 1978 nearly doubled 1977's, and 1979's tally peaked at roughly 78,000. Another 68,595 Fiestas were sold in the U.S. in 1980 before the relatively peppy economy car was dropped in favor of the new Escort then waiting in the wings.

ABOVE: *The European model of the Ford Fiesta*

Engine: *97.6 cubic-inch four-cylinder*

Suspension: *MacPherson struts and front-wheel-drive half shafts up front, solid beam axle with Panhard rod and trailing links in back*

Price: *$3,680*

Wheelbase: *90 inches*

Weight: *1,550 pounds*

Model availability: *two-door compact sedan*

Production: *40,549*

1979 Mustang Indy 500 Pace Car

Time tends to march on, and so did the Mustang. Plans for an all-new third-generation ponycar were forming even as the Pinto-based Mustang IIs were moving out showroom doors at a pace comparable to their first-generation forerunners. Initially mentioned in Ford Motor Company paperwork in February 1973, the "Fox" chassis project involved two lines of fuel-efficient models. Henry Ford II and Lee Iacocca gave the go-ahead to the Fox project in December 1974, leading to the eventual arrival of Ford's Fairmont and Mercury's Zephyr in August 1977. A Mustang/Capri version of the Fox chassis was also in the works but was delayed a year, leaving the new third-generation ponycar to debut as a 1979 model. The Fairmont-based, Fox-

chassis Mustang wore an attractive shell fashioned by Jack Telnack's styling team. There were two body styles: a coupe and a hatchback. The new chassis featured a coil-spring, four-link rear suspension and MacPherson struts up front. Standard power in 1979 came from a 2.3-liter four-cylinder, but an optional 2.3-liter turbocharged four and a

130-horsepower 5.0-liter (302 cubic inches) V8 hinted, that just maybe performance was returning to Ford's ponycar corral. In the opinion of *Motor Trend's* John Ethridge, the 1979 Mustang could "now compete both in the marketplace and on the road with lots of cars that used to outclass it."

aluminum wheels, Michelin metric rubber and specially tuned springs and shocks.

Like its forerunner 15 years before, the 1979 Mustang was chosen as the prestigious pace car for the annual running of the Indianapolis 500. After the 48th running of the Indy 500 in May 1964, Dearborn offered roughly 200 identically equipped pace car replica coupes to the lucky few customers able to snatch them up. Street-going replicas were again released in 1979, but this time they

SPECIFICATIONS

Engine: *140-horsepower turbocharged OHV four-cylinder 140-horsepower 302 cubic-inch OHV V8*

Price: *$9,000 (with 5.0L V8)*

Wheelbase: *100.4 inches*

Length: *179.1 inches*

Weight: *2,900 pounds*

Model availability: *two-door hatchback*

Construction: *unitized body/frame with isolated front subframe*

Suspension: *MacPherson strut in front, four-bar link and coil springs in back*

Brakes: *front discs, rear drums*

Production: *10,478*

Even though it was wider, longer and taller than its forerunners, the first Fox-chassis Mustang was 200 pounds lighter than the Mustang II. Popular options in 1979 included the Cobra graphics package and the TRX sport suspension, the latter featuring attractive

were a bit easier to come by. Interestingly, it was another 15 years before a ponycar from Ford again paced the 500, and the honor helped mark yet another all-new Mustang as the Fox-chassis legacy came to a close in 1993.

1981-90: Return of the Red, White and Blue Oval

"Henry Ford II did not exactly fulfill his early-1970s promise of running the foreign cars and trucks right 'back into the sea.' By 1982 imports were still eating up nearly 30 per cent of the market. But that was the high-water mark."

When Lee Iacocca left Ford in 1978 the corporation was in the middle of its best six-month profit run ever. Perhaps a bit too full of himself, Iacocca then predicted that Dearborn might never see such rich cash flow again. He was wrong; record profits would return soon enough—but not after some truly lean times.

The really bad year of 1980 was followed up by another tough one in 1981, when the company lost $1.06 billion and production dipped below one million for the first time since the recession-wracked days of 1958. Fortunately for Ford, everyone in Detroit was in the same boat (as they had been in 1958 as well), and all once again benefited when rough economic waters soon settled. America's latest recession hit rock bottom in 1982, a year in which Ford "only" lost $658 million and total industry sales dropped to the lowest they had been in two decades.

Happy days did return again, however. Total industry sales reversed themselves in 1984, topping $10 billion, a plateau last reached in 1979. This upward trend continued unabated, resulting in big dollars for the Big Three. Ford profits for 1984 hit a record of $2.91 billion, a short-lived standard broken again in 1987 when the corporation made $4.63 billion, and again the following year when the tally reached $5.3 billion. But the really big news had come in 1986 as Ford Motor Company's profits topped GM's for the first time since 1924. Ford remained number one from a dollar-sign perspective in 1987 and 1988, and its market share that last year (nearly 21.6 per cent) was its highest dating back to 1979.

What made the difference? How did Ford turn the ship around in such short order? Finally catching on to just how fat they had grown during the 1960s and 1970s—a lesson taught hard to Americans by the Japanese—was the key to their newly discovered success seen all around Detroit by the mid-1980s. In Ford's case, increasing efficiency and workmanship at all its plants and better targeting of its products while keeping a close eye on the future were prime factors behind its consecutive record-shattering sale years.

ABOVE: *The 1982 EXP hatchback coupe was a part of Project "Erica" that produced the Escort series, first of Ford's line of "World Cars."*

ABOVE: *A 1989 Mustang LX convertible is closely scrutinized by Ford Quality Control personnel as it nears the end of the line at the Dearborn Assembly Plant.*

"How did Ford turn the ship around in such short order? Finally catching on to just how fat they had grown during the 1960s and 1970s— a lesson taught hard to Americans by the Japanese—was the key to their newly discovered success."

But like all its rivals, Dearborn also had received a little help from Washington in 1981 in the form of the Voluntary Restraint Agreement, which temporarily limited Japanese imports to the U.S. in order to give this county's auto industry a chance to catch up with their overseas competitors. Relaxing CAFE ratings a few years later also contributed a bit of breathing room for a group of automakers who all claimed that 27.5 mpg was an unreasonable goal for 1985. Lee Iacocca had perhaps complained the loudest concerning the tightening emissions standards while still at Ford.

Most Detroit executives took advantage of these opportunities and did not look back, although they did not necessarily beat the Japanese as much as they joined them. Adopting their manufacturing practices and matching them car for car was just the beginning. By the decade's end, various joint-ventures between the countries would be in full swing, with Ford having hooked up with Mazda, GM with Isuzu, and Chrysler with Mitsubishi. Henry Ford II did not exactly fulfill his early-1970s promise of running the foreign cars and trucks right "back into the sea." By 1982 imports were still eating up nearly 30 per cent of the market, but that was the high-water mark.

ABOVE: *A 1984 GT350 is pictured here with a 'Sixty-four-and-a-half' convertible.*

ABOVE: *Race driver Bill Elliottt (left) meets Robert Patterson, owner of the one millionth T-Bird, a 1972 model, seen here behind the "new" 1987 Turbo Coupe.*

Revitalized competitive measures on the product front included a rash of new downsized models introduced during the 1980s: Escort in 1981, Tempo in 1984, the Aerostar minivan and popular Taurus in 1986, the Mazda-based Probe in 1989. In 1983 Dearborn entered the mini-truck race in full-force with its new compact Ranger pickup, a true-blue, "all-American" replacement for the little Mazda-built Courier that had been marketed by Ford since 1972. The Ranger was then joined by the equally compact Bronco II sport-utility vehicle in 1984.

Top management at Ford also went through various changes during the 1980s, with some names being new, others not so. First came Henry Ford II's retirement as chairman in 1982. In his place went former president Philip Caldwell, making this the first time in Ford Motor Company history that the man at the top did not share the "name on the building." Replacing Caldwell, who had been president since Iacocca's firing in 1978, was Donald Petersen, a true "car guy" who had been at Ford since 1949. Petersen then moved up to the top spot after Caldwell's retirement in 1985, and he remained on the throne until he too retired in 1990, opening the door for Harold "Red" Poling.

In the meantime, William Clay Ford, Sr., had resigned as vice president in 1989, meaning no one named Ford remained in the upper echelons of the corporation with the same name. But it was clear that the bloodline was not to end there. One year before, in January 1988, both Henry II's son, Edsel Ford II, and his cousin, William Clay Ford, Jr., had both taken positions on the firm's board of directors, making it clear that future plans involved keeping the company firmly in the family.

1982 Ford EXP

Ford officials had wowed America with their sporty two-seat Thunderbird in 1955 but had then gone on to disappoint many avid T-bird fanatics across the land when they added room for two more passengers in the back in 1958. A true two-seater from Dearborn would not be reintroduced into the Ford stables for nearly a quarter of a century.

Introduced in April 1981 as a 1982 model, Ford's sporty EXP was a breath of fresh air that company officials unashamedly tried to compare with those early successful Thunderbirds. "We're introducing another two-seater with the same flair [as the 1955-57 Thunderbird], but the EXP will be a very affordable, very fuel efficient car matched to the lifestyles of the Eighties," announced the division general manager Louis E Latalf.

Indeed, many who saw the first EXP at the Chicago Auto Show in the spring were impressed with the way that this intriguing two-seat hatchback disguised its rather humble Escort heritage. Longer, lower and shorter than the Escort, the EXP featured an aggressive-looking body that, at the very least, traded the Escort's boxy form for fast-looking lines. Some critics felt that the front end was a rather poor copy of Austin-Healey's "bug-eye" Sprite, but then you cannot please everyone.

Unfortunately, the first EXP did not please many customers with its performance, thanks to the fact that the Escort's weak-kneed 70-horsepower four-cylinder carried over with absolutely no disguise whatsover.

Though this was a trick set-up, unfortunately it could not hide the car's under-powered nature. By the time engineers addressed complaints concerning the car's sluggish ways—with an 80-horsepower upgrade, which was introduced in March 1982—it was basically too late. Ford did manage to sell nearly 100,000 EXP hatchbacks that first year (while Mercury moved 35,000 of its similar LN7 "bubbleback" coupes), the die was cast. The EXP's first year was also its best. Its popularity very quickly dwindled, leading to the car's cancellation in 1988.

SPECIFICATIONS

Engine: 70-horsepower 1.6-liter (97.6 cubic inches) overhead-cam four-cylinder with aluminum head; 80-horsepower version introduced in March 1982

Compression: 8.7:1 (70-horse version); 9.0:1 (80-horse version)

Bore & stroke: 3.15 x 3.13 inches

Transmission: four-speed manual transaxle, standard

Suspension: independent MacPherson struts with coil springs and lower control arm, front; independent trailing links with MacPherson struts and coil springs, rear

Brakes: front discs, rear drums

Price: $7,387

Wheelbase: 94.2 inches

Weight: 2,047 pounds

Model availability: three-door hatchback coupe

Construction: unitized body/frame with front-wheel drive

Production: 98,256

1984-86 SVO Mustang

Performance had become a dirty word around Detroit during the 1970s as building cleaner-running, fuel-efficient vehicles took top priority with all automakers at the time. As for factory-backed racing, no one had slammed the door shut on that venture with more emphasis than Henry Ford II had in late 1970.

Then along came the 1980s and new leadership was introduced to Dearborn, infusing the Ford Motor Company with new inspiration and ideas that changed the direction of the company yet again, and worked to reinvigorate customer interest and investment. Under president Donald Petersen's direction, Ford engineers found it fun to build cars again. Their Fox-chassis Mustang, which had replaced the disappointing Mustang II in 1979, represented the first turn in the right direction as far as performance-conscious customers were concerned. Next came a new company division for Ford that was dedicated to putting the Blue Oval back in action at the race track.

Announced in September 1980, Ford's Special Vehicle Operations department was formed to create "a series of limited-production performance cars and develop their image through motorsport." Michael Kranefuss, who had previously been competition director for Ford of Europe, was brought in from across the Atlantic to run the the new division, and he wasted little time in putting the latest-generation ponycar to work on IMSA and SCCA road-racing courses. As for a "limited-production performance car" for the street, that long-rumored model finally came along nearly four years later.

A major blast of fresh air, the 1984 SVO Mustang wowed critics with its hot performance and Euro-style sporty flair. Beneath its asymmetrical hood scoop was an intercooled, turbocharged engine that pumped out V8-type horsepower using only four cylinders. Output for this 140 cubic-inch (2.3 liter) four was an amazing 175 horses. Throw in a Hurst-shifted five-speed manual transmission, Koni gas-charged shocks absorbers, quick-ratio steering, four-wheel disc brakes and 16-inch aluminum wheels, and the sum of the parts

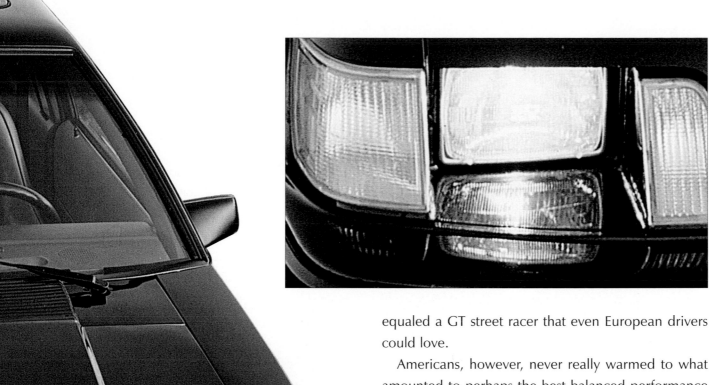

equaled a GT street racer that even European drivers could love.

Americans, however, never really warmed to what amounted to perhaps the best balanced performance Mustang to date, a claim echoed by more than one automotive magazine nearly 20 years back. Such raves did not translate into sufficient sales, even after engineers bumped the output up to 205 horsepower for the 1985 SVO Mustang. The innovative machine was cancelled in 1986 after 9,844 were built for the disappointingly short, three-year run.

That the SVO Mustang came and went in such a rush was not necessarily the car's fault. Ford officials later admitted that making muscle, not marketing it, was the Special Vehicle Operations department's forte. A better balanced business approach would come along in the 1990s to promote an even better breed of hot-to-trot Mustang.

This time the new name on the office door would be "Special Vehicle Team."

SPECIFICATIONS

Engine: 2.3-liter SOHC inline four-cylinder

Bore & stroke: 3.78 x 3.12 inches

Compression: 8.0:1

Output: 175 horsepower in 1984, 205 horsepower in 1985, 200 horsepower in 1986

Fuel delivery: intercooled turbocharger with electronic fuel injection

Suspension: independent MacPherson struts with coil springs and Koni gas-charged shocks, front; four-link solid axle with coil springs and Koni gas-charged shocks, rear

Steering: quick-ratio rack and pinion with power assist

Brakes: four-wheel discs

Price: $16,000

Wheelbase: 100.5 inches

Weight: 3,040 pounds

Model availability: two-door hatchback coupe

Construction: unitized body/frame

Production: 9,844 for 1984-86

1984 Lincoln Mk VII LSC

Perhaps the sexiest-looking Lincoln since the Mk II of 1956-57, the Mk VII coupe debuted as a 1984 model year, with new "contemporary dimensions" and a sleek, sporty shell that favored function every bit as much as form. According to promotional people, the easier-to-handle, downsized Mk VII was "the most airflow-efficient luxury car built in America." Drag coefficient for its "more personal" two-door coupe body was a slippery 0.38, a major plus as far as both fuel-efficiency and performance were concerned.

As for the latter, a new options group also appeared for 1984 to help transform the sensational-looking Mk VII into a "hot rod Lincoln." The LSC group included a special handling package, quick-ratio power steering, a 3.27:1 rear axle ratio, and

aggressive P215/65R15 Goodyear Eagle GT tires mounted on eye-catching 15x6 aluminum wheels. Foglamps, dark charcoal accent paint for the lower bodysides, and leather appointments inside added to the appeal. Even the LSC's trunk area was "upgraded."

Remaining LSC engineering was standard Mk VII material, which was not a bad thing. Rack and pinion steering, four-wheel discs, a four-speed automatic overdrive gearbox and the proven 5.0-liter V8 were all present and accounted for, as was Detroit's first electronically

controlled air suspension system that was developed in conjunction with Goodyear. The system consisted of four air springs, a compressor, three height sensors and a microprocessor, that all worked to maintain a constant ride height.

The idea behind this revolutionary concept was to give a ride quality equal to that of the bigger Lincolns of yesterday, but with far superior handling. The Mark VII was also the first American car with flush-glazed headlamps, made legal just before the model went into production. These European-style aero headlamps were opposed by federal government to begin with, but Ford won approval for them after a two-year battle. A turbocharged six cylinder diesel engine was then offered as an alternative to the standard 5.0-liter V8 for

the first time, and sales for the Lincoln saw a massive rise of a 31 per cent.

The sum of all these parts represented perhaps America's most exciting luxury car for many years, a classy cruiser that Ford Motor Company officials hoped would run right up with the growing group of European sport sedans then gaining favor in America. It was over a foot shorter and nearly 400 pounds lighter than its predessor the Mark VI.

LSC Lincolns were offered up through 1992 then reappeared mid-year in 1995 for the even sleeker Mk VIII, introduced in 1993.

SPECIFICATIONS

Engine: *140-horsepower 5.0-liter (302 cubic inches) OHV V8*

Bore & stroke: *4.00 x 3.00*

Compression: *8.4:1*

Fuel delivery: *Throttle-body electronic fuel injection*

Transmission: *four-speed automatic overdrive*

Steering: *rack and pinion with quick-ratio power assist*

Suspension: *MacPherson struts in front; four-link solid axle in rear; electronic auto-leveling air springs and gas-charged shock absorbers at all four wheels*

Brakes: *four-wheel discs*

Price: *$23,706*

Wheelbase: *108.5 inches*

Length: *202.8 inches*

Width: *70.9 inches*

Weight: *3,700 pounds*

Model availability: *two-door, five-passenger coupe*

1985 Merkur XR4Ti

Born in 1985, Mercury's XR4Ti picked up where the sporty little Capri had left off in 1977. Like the imported Capri, the XR4Ti was an "Americanized" version of a popular European-market compact, in this case the Ford Sierra XR4i hatchback, introduced across the Atlantic in 1983. The sporty Sierra XR4I had evolved from the Probe III showcar, itself unveiled at the Frankfurt Auto Show in 1981.

On Lincoln-Mercury showroom floors in America, the imported XR4Ti wore the new "Merkur" badge as part of a new L-M strategy that, according to company officials, represented a response to American car buyers' quests for "distinguished vehicles of European heritage." In the XR4Ti, Euro-wannabes in the West found a relatively comfortable five-passenger sport sedan that, unlike most contemporary compacts of the day, still relied on "traditional"rear-wheel-drive.

Four-wheel independent suspension, front disc brakes and a turbocharged, fuel-injected, four-cylinder engine with twin, overhead camshafts, were standard. Included in the deal was a suitably sporting, five-speed, manual gearbox with a three-speed automatic available as an option. Standard equipment included a high-profile "biplane" rear spoiler, lower body cladding, halogen headlights and foglamps, and bright, stylish aluminum-alloy wheels shod in Pirelli tires. Braking was provided by a front disc/rear drum set-up that coped with the car's performance more than adequately. The rack and pinion steering was equipped with a variable power assist system that retained the sporting feel of the car at speed, whilst allowing it to be parked effortlessly.

The XR4Ti certainly looked the part of a sport sedan, and the driver experience behind the wheel did not disappoint, either. Nonetheless, the hot, little compact never did really catch on in America. It did develop its own devoted, equally small following, but sales never amounted to much. Though the Merkur line carried on for a while, Lincoln-Mercury dropped the XR4Ti after 1989.

1986 Ford Taurus

This was a year for serious celebration around Dearborn, thanks primarily to the introduction of two truly new models from Ford and Mercury. Named Taurus and Sable, respectively, these two sensationally sleek Euro-style sedans simply stole the attention of both car buyers and critics. The two finished well ahead of the pack in *Motor Trend*'s annual "Car of the Year" competition, with Taurus narrowly nudging out Sable for the coveted trophy. *Motor Trend*'s John Hanson wrote, while announcing 1986's winner, "Ford has somehow managed to step away from the stodgy Detroit establishment of sameness, and design a car of the future."

Middle-class customers snatched up Ford's fancy front-wheel-drive family car, forcing the Chicago and Atlanta plants into overtime to keep the supply going. Ultimately the new Taurus ranked as the sixth-best seller on the domestic car leader board for 1986.

The Taurus was a great buy any way you looked at it. Beneath that beautiful body was a roomy,

comfortable six-passenger transporter priced well below various trendy European sedans then turning heads in America. A frugal four-cylinder engine was standard, but a peppy V6 could have been added at extra cost to help that slippery shell slide through the wind with ease. Jack Telnack's design team made sure all that aerodynamic styling did not just look the part—at 0.32, the Taurus sedan's drag coefficient ranked right up with the world's best.

Nearly 20 years later, Taurus is still running well ahead of the rest and selling like nobody's business. From 1987 to 2001, annual sales totals failed to surpass 300,000 only once—in 1991 when the figure was 299,659. For five straight years, 1992 to 1996, Taurus ranked as America's best-selling car.

Yet another reason to celebrate then came on October 23, 2002, as employees at Ford's Atlanta plant all stopped work to watch as the six millionth Taurus rolled off the line. Such long-running success stories are few and far between in Detroit these days.

SPECIFICATIONS

Engine: 88-horsepower 2.5-liter OHV inline four-cylinder, standard 140-horsepower 3.0-liter OHV V6, optional

Transmission: three-speed automatic transaxle

Steering: rack and pinion

Suspension: independent MacPherson struts with coil springs and lower control arms, front: independent MacPherson struts with coil spring, rear

Brakes: front discs, rear drums

Price: $9,645 to $13,860

Wheelbase: 106 inches

Weight: 3,620 pounds

Model availability: four-door sedan and four-door station wagon, both of six-passenger capacity

Construction: unitized body/frame with front-wheel drive

Production: 178,737 sedans, 57,625 station wagons

1986 Ford Aerostar Minivan

The pre-cursor to today's wildly popular SUV was the cute, little minivan, first popularized by Chrysler 20 years ago. Before the Dodge Caravan and Plymouth Voyager came along late in 1983, the concept of a relatively lightweight, affordable passenger van was basically unproven in America, though Volkswagen did make more than one hippie happy during the 1960s. As late as 1983, minivan sales still only constituted a scant one per cent of the American truck market.

That figure then rose to 9.9 per cent in 1985, the year Ford entered the minivan race with its Aerostar. Introduced that summer as a 1986 model, the

Aerostar looked and felt larger than its Caravan rival. But its base price was $200 less than the both the Dodge and Chevrolet's Astro van, unveiled in 1984. Like Astro, Ford's Aerostar relied on a front-engine, rear-drive platform. The Astro,

however, came standard with V6 power. The Aerostar's base engine was an inline four, with a V6 available at extra cost—thus the difference in bottom lines.

second. But by that time a new breed of utility vehicle was turning soccer moms' heads. And this time it was Ford that got the jump out of the blocks.

SPECIFICATIONS

Engine: 90-horsepower 2.3-liter OHV inline four-cylinder, standard

Bore & stroke: 3.78 x 3.13 inches

Fuel delivery: electronic fuel injection

Transmission: five-speed manual, standard

Steering: rack and pinion

Brakes: front discs, rear drums

Price: $9,398

Wheelbase: 118.9 inches

Length: 174.9 inches

Weight: 3,620 pounds

Model availability: three-door mini-van

Production: 143,745

With its headstart, Chrysler dominated the minivan market into the 1990s, with Ford running in third behind General Motors. It was not until 1993 that Dearborn officials finally found themselves in

1989 Ford Probe

Mustang fans are a devoted lot, which helps explain why Ford still has a ponycar up and running in 2003 and GM does not. Chevrolet's Camaro and Pontiac's Firebird simply could not keep pace with the rolling legend that had started it all back in 1964 and thus were killed off. As we speak, Dearborn designers are putting the finishing touches on yet another next-generation Mustang, while Detroit-watchers are left wondering just what a reincarnated Camaro will look like—and you can bet your bow-tie that the nameplate will return. Whether or not that will be a good thing remains to be seen.

If not for its fanatical following, Mustang too might have experienced its own

rebirth 15 years ago. As early as 1982, Ford planners had begun work on a future replacement for the Fox-chassis platform, then only three years old. The initial project, labeled "SN-8," called for a frugal (yet sporty) front-wheel-drive compact priced a bit below the existing Mustang. To make the SN-8 ideal a reality, Dearborn officials turned to their joint-venture partners from Japan, Mazda, a firm experienced in

the art of fuel-efficient front-wheel-drive. The two companies from opposite sides of the world had a working prototype rolling by 1985, and word soon leaked out that it would replace the Mustang in 1988 or 1989.

"Not so fast" came the response from the Blue Oval faithful, who bombed Dearborn with letters of protest. Dealers too complained about the proposed front-driven "Mazstang," as did critics in the automotive press. "The descendants of the 1979 Mustang, namely the GTs, pulled the Mustang name out of the ditch that was dug by the Mustang II," wrote *Mustang Monthly* magazine's Donald Farr. "And now, after the Mustang has clawed

its way to the top of the ponycar heap once again, Ford plans to turn it into a front-wheel-drive copy of a Japanese car. Un-American, I say."

The disapproving din was so loud Ford officials could not help but hear. Then they acted. In August 1987, they announced that the new platform would debut under a new name: Probe. The Fox-chassis Mustang would carry on, though with few changes up until 1993 due to the fact that no work on an update had begun until after the decision had been made to run with the Probe.

Sharing most of its mechanics with Mazda's own MX-6 sport coupe, the front-wheel-drive Probe debuted in the summer of 1988 as a 1989 model. While this attractive coupe did develop its own following it was certainly no substitute for the car that so many Americans have loved now for more than 30 years. For once an automaker listened to its customers—and both parties came out winners.

SPECIFICATIONS

Engine: 110-horsepower 2.2-liter Mazda-supplied four-cylinder with three valves per cylinder

Bore & stroke: 3.39 x 3.7 inches

Fuel delivery: electronic multiport fuel injection

Transmission: five-speed manual transaxle, standard

Steering: rack and pinion with power assist

Suspension: independent struts with coil springs, front; independent trailing links and coils springs, rear

Brakes: front discs, rear drums, with power assist (four-wheel discs standard for Probe GT)

Price: ranged from $10,459 to $13,593

Wheelbase: 99 inches

Weight: 2,715 pounds

Model availability: two-door four-passenger compact coupe in three trim levels; GL, LX and GT

Construction: unitized body/frame with front-wheel drive

Production: 162,889

1991-2000: By Any Other Name

"Our goal now is to provide personal mobility for everyone— including future generationsby making it economically, environmentally and socially sustainable over time."

BELOW: *The 1994, 302-cubic inch (5 liter) Mustang V8 could produce 240 bhp in S-Cobra form.*

Henry Ford supposedly gave up the leadership of the company that bore his name to his son Edsel in 1919, although anyone with eyes could see that the younger Ford was little more than a puppet. Old Henry would not let go of the reigns, no matter how rocky the road, almost right up to his death. With the help of the Ford women, Edsel's son, Henry Ford II, managed to wrestle control away from his grizzled grandfather's clenches in 1944 to both save the firm from ruin and continue its family-run tradition. That tradition then carried on for nearly 40 years before someone other than a Ford finally took a seat atop the corporation.

First Philip Caldwell then Donald Petersen directed Ford through its soaring rebirth in the 1980s. But Petersen opted out of the top office in 1990, leaving the throne to Red Poling until his retirement in 1993. Alex Trotman rose to the top next. Then five years later came the news many Detroit-watchers had been waiting to hear for more than a decade. In September 1998, another Ford man was elected chairman of the fabled firm then nearing its 100th anniversary. Only 41, William Clay Ford, Jr., took office on January 1, 1999, was then named CEO in October 2001. Apparently everything old is new again. Almost everything.

"Ford Motor Company put the world on wheels by making personal mobility affordable," said William Clay, Jr., right after he was appointed CEO. "Our goal now is to provide personal mobility for everyone—including future generations—by making it economically, environmentally and socially sustainable over time. We want to have an even greater impact on the world in our next 100 years than we did in our last 100."

"A lifelong environmentalist," according to press release words, Bill Ford is accustomed to modern problems his great-

ABOVE: *The last hurrah—a racing Thunderbird competes in the 1997 NASCAR series.*

"I believe business goals can best be achieved by also addressing social and environmental needs"

Bill Ford

RIGHT: *The 1995 Mutang GT and GTS were fitted with the 215 bhp version of the 302 V8.*

"Companies that can react quickly to emerging issues will be able to turn them into marketplace advantage, and everyone will benefit."

Bill Ford

ABOVE: *The identity plate on this 1997 Thunderbird indicates that it was the very last one built—until the new one was exhibited a couple of years later at the 1999 Detroit Auto Show!*

grandfather never had to face. "I believe business goals can best be achieved by also addressing social and environmental needs," he continued. "Companies that can react quickly to emerging issues will be able to turn them into marketplace advantage, and everyone will benefit."

A Princeton graduate with a masters of science degree in management from MIT, Bill Ford joined Ford Motor Company in 1979 as a product-planning analyst. Various other positions followed, allowing him to gain valuable experience in everything from finance, to marketing, to manufacturing, to labor relations. He was clearly being groomed for the top, as was his cousin, Edsel Ford II, who had joined Ford earlier in 1974, also as a product analyst.

Some witnesses, both inside Ford and out, were more than curious after the two young men were elevated to board of director positions in 1988 as part of an obviously continuing plan to "teach them the ropes." In that group was a slightly rankled Donald Petersen, who told *Fortune*

LEFT: *The 2000 Mustang Cobra R, with twin, overhead camshafts and over 300 bhp, put the Mustang back where it had been prior to the oil crises of the early 1970s—on top of the pile.*

RIGHT: *The well-packed engine compartment of the 1994 Mustang Cobra 5.0 liter—a 305-cubic inch V8, tuned to 240 bhp. A 351-cubic inch V8, producing 300bhp, would debut the following year.*

BELOW: *The 1994 Mustang GT. In 1994, the Mustang came close to outselling the Chevrolet Camaro and the Pontiac Firebird combined, with over 137,000 units being produced.*

magazine in 1989 that "I'm not a caretaker for anybody." Continued Petersen, "the principle we must operate on is that selection to top management is based solely on merit." No problem: William Ford, Jr., simply went on to prove he could handle the top job.

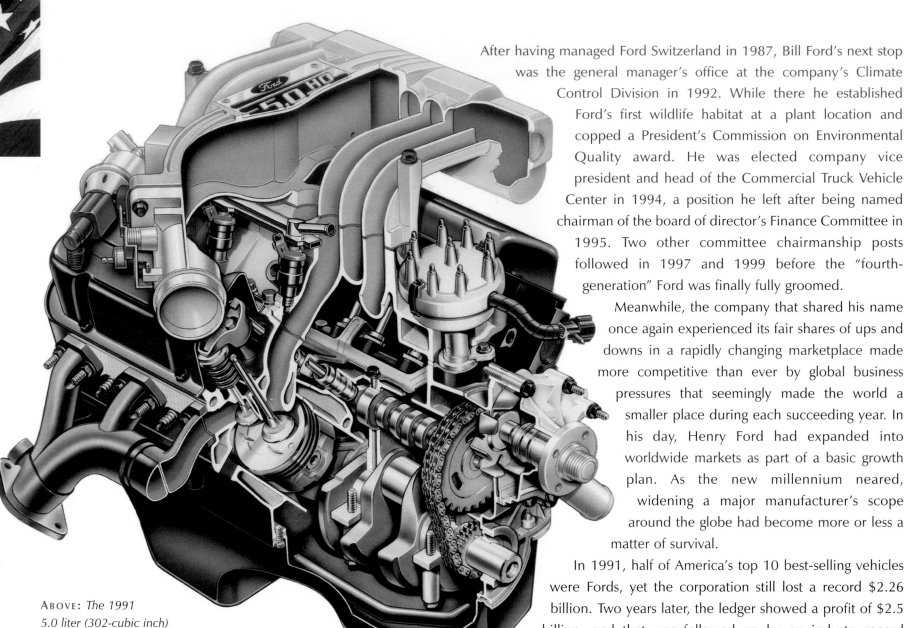

After having managed Ford Switzerland in 1987, Bill Ford's next stop was the general manager's office at the company's Climate Control Division in 1992. While there he established Ford's first wildlife habitat at a plant location and copped a President's Commission on Environmental Quality award. He was elected company vice president and head of the Commercial Truck Vehicle Center in 1994, a position he left after being named chairman of the board of director's Finance Committee in 1995. Two other committee chairmanship posts followed in 1997 and 1999 before the "fourth-generation" Ford was finally fully groomed.

Meanwhile, the company that shared his name once again experienced its fair shares of ups and downs in a rapidly changing marketplace made more competitive than ever by global business pressures that seemingly made the world a smaller place during each succeeding year. In his day, Henry Ford had expanded into worldwide markets as part of a basic growth plan. As the new millennium neared, widening a major manufacturer's scope around the globe had become more or less a matter of survival.

In 1991, half of America's top 10 best-selling vehicles were Fords, yet the corporation still lost a record $2.26 billion. Two years later, the ledger showed a profit of $2.5 billion, and that was followed up by an industry-record $5.308 billion in 1994. A roller-coaster ride, indeed.

ABOVE: *The 1991 5.0 liter (302-cubic inch) HO V8, as employed in the Thunderbird and the Mercury Cougar XR7, could produce 225 bhp.*

"As the new millennium neared, widening a major manufacturer's scope around the globe had become more or less a matter of survival."

To gain a more solid footing both in the U.S. and on the international business stage, Alex Trotman's team in 1995 initiated their "Ford 2000" program, which aimed "to combine the power, resources and reach of a world company with the immediacy, intimacy, agility and spirit of a small one." Trotman had prefaced the Ford 2000 plan in 1994 with the merger of Ford's North American and European operations and its Automotive Components Group into a new single structure named Ford Automotive Operations, a simplification that reportedly would save as much as $3 billion a year. It then became the goal of the five-year Ford 2000 project to cut, trim, streamline and consolidate the company's worldwide affairs into a lean, mean competition-eating machine.

Additional outside firms were also snatched up along the way to help widen the corporation's scope. Ford bought out the remaining shares of Aston Martin Lagonda,

RIGHT: *The 1998 Escort ZX-2 clearly shows the homogenization of the company's European and Domestic model ranges.*

BELOW: *The 1995 Ranger Splash continued Ford's tradition of producing durable, no-nonsense, practical pick-ups that had been established with the Model T.*

ABOVE: *The 1996 Ford Taurus LX Station Wagon cost over $22,000 and faced stiff competition from foreign imports and cheaper domestic alternatives.*

Ltd., in 1994 after gaining 75 per cent of the British firm in 1987. Another British legend, Jaguar, was snatched up in 1990, and Volvo joined the fold in 1999. Kia and Mazda from the Far East too revolve in the Ford universe, as do various Ford affiliates in various countries from India to South America.

It certainly looks like William Clay Ford, Jr., now has the whole world in his hands, and he certainly has his hands full.

1991 Ford Explorer

Ford people did not invent the SUV, it more or less evolved over many years, but they can claim coinage of the term. When the compact Bronco debuted for 1966, it was originally offered in three models: Roadster, Wagon and "Sports Utility." Though quickly forgotten, that last label later resurfaced (without the "s" at the end of "sport") as a generic reference for all the refined trucks that burst onto the scene in the 1990s to steal away customers from the car side of the market. These new "sport-utility vehicles" combined the practicality of a light-duty pickup with much of the comfort and convenience of a typical family sedan. Throw in optional four-wheel-drive and you had all the bases covered. Why own both a car and a truck when you could have the best of both worlds all wrapped up under one roof?

The modern SUV's roots run as far back as 1935, when Chevrolet introduced its passenger-friendly Suburban. Later milestones include International's Travelall, born in 1956, and Kaiser-Jeep's Wagoneer, created in 1963. But if you ask most soccer moms today which company is most responsible for making their lives easier, the answer is Ford.

Forget about the light-weight minivan, that was an Eighties thing. When the new Explorer appeared in the spring of 1990 as a 1991 model, both car- and truck-buyers alike were drawn into Ford dealerships like insects to a 100-watt bulb. The Explorer instantly became the runaway

two- and four-door forms, it was roomier and much more refined than the Bronco it replaced. Three classy trim packages were offered, including the upscale "Eddie Bauer" edition, and the options list was as long as most cars'. The longer four-door Explorer was understandably more popular, as was the 4x4 version. Optional four-wheel-drive was ordered on 74 per cent of the Explorers delivered that first year.

True to its name, Ford's Explorer blazed a trail through the 1990s for all other rivals to follow. In 2002 it was still America's best-selling SUV.

SPECIFICATIONS

Engine: *155-horsepower 245 cubic-inch OHV V6*

Bore & stroke: *3.95 x 3.32 inches*

Compressions: *9.0:1*

Fuel delivery: *electronically controlled fuel injection*

Transmission: *five-speed manual, standard*

Price: *ranged from $14,926 to $17,694*

Wheelbase: *102.1 inches, two-door; 111.9 inches, four-door*

Weight: *ranged from 3,681 pounds to 4,012 pounds*

Model availability: *two- and four-door _one-ton "Wagon" with two- or four-wheel drive*

Construction: *body on frame*

Production: *322,328*

leader of the fledgling SUV market, and by March 1991 it was the seventh best-selling vehicle, car or truck, in America.

Sure, it was more or less a Ranger mini-pickup with a Bronco II-style body in back. But Explorer was by no means just a truck with a roof over its bed. Offered in

1993 Lincoln Mk VIII

Yet another restyled Lincoln coupe debuted in 1993, and once again it wowed luxury buyers with its sleek, sporty lines. Even more aerodynamic than its predecessor, the new Mk VIII made the highly acclaimed Mk VII look boxy in comparison. Soft contours replaced sharp edges and its overall stance appeared as long and low as ever. That stance got even lower as the driver's right foot grew heavier thanks to an innovative speed-sensitive height adjustment system. The air springs at the corners automatically dropped the Mk VIII an additional 0.8 inches whenever the speedometer read 55 mph or more for longer than 45 seconds.

The 1993 Mk VIII's power source was a 280-horsepower variation on Ford Motor Company's modular-motor theme. Of all aluminum construction, this 4.6-liter V8 featured dual overhead cams and

sequential fuel injection. It was backed by a techno-trick 4R70W four-speed automatic overdrive transmission. Four-wheel anti-lock discs and micropressor-controlled self-leveling air springs were also supplied as standard specifications.

Inside, the Mk VIII featured dual air bags, a leather-wrapped steering wheel, and a programmable memory driver's seat. Popular options included a JBL stereo, power moonroof, leather bucket seats, an overhead console, illuminated keyless entry and the ever-present cellular car phone.

One optional group not offered for the 1993 Mk VIII was the LSC sport package, which last appeared on the 1992 Mk VII. But fortunately, for those who love the prestige and performance all wrapped up together, the LSC Lincoln did reappear midyear (with 10 extra horses) for 1995 Mk VIII customers. The car was warmly welcomed back.

SPECIFICATIONS

Engine: *280-horsepower 4.6-liter DOHC "mod-motor" V8*

Bore & stroke: *3.60 x 3.60 inches*

Compression: *9.8:1*

Fuel delivery: *sequential fuel injection*

Transmission: *four-speed automatic overdrive transmission*

Steering: *rack and pinion with speed-sensitive power assist*

Suspension: *independent control-arms with coil springs, front; indepentent control-arms with coil springs, rear; self-leveling air springs, front and rear*

Brakes: *four-wheel discs with power assist*

Price: *$36,640*

Wheelbase: *113 inches*

Length: *206.9 inches*

Width: *73.9 inches*

Height: *53.6 inches*

Weight: *3,741 pounds*

Model availability: *two-door, four-passenger coupe*

Construction: *unitized body/frame*

Production: *30,899*

1994 Mustang GT

Ford's Fox-chassis Mustang survived for 15 years, five more than planned. Though devoted followers were delighted when the Probe did not supercede the car of their dreams in 1989, Dearborn designers knew they could not carry on much

longer with a platform that was growing a bit tired. There were few notable changes on Mustangs between 1987 and 1993.

Then came 1994 and a rebirth of sorts that promised a continuing bright future and reminded many of a historic past. "The wonderful changes that have been made in this automobile will, we feel, bring back this country's love affair with the Mustang," said program manager Mike Zevalkink. "We brought back a lot of the Mustang

heritage in a very contemporary way," added design manager Bud Magaldi. "That seemed to be what people wanted us to do. They didn't want another 1964-1/2 or 1965 Mustang, which they loved. They wanted a new car." Reportedly 1,330 of the car's 1,850 parts were making their debut in 1994. "This is not a carryover platform," said Will Boddie, Ford's Small and Midsize Car Segment director. After spending $700 million on the car and its assembly plant, Ford started building the 1994 Mustang in October 1993.

Underneath was a new chassis, a rigid foundation that improved steering, ride and handling, and also did away with much of the twists and shakes common to the previous platform. A slightly longer wheelbase and wider tread also contributed to the car's newfound confidence. Standard four-wheel discs enhanced the attraction even further, as did a 145-horsepower V6 in place of the old four-cylinder in base models. The tried-and-true 5.0 small-block, now rated at 215 horsepower, remained for the GT.

Another terrific engine arrived in 1996 as the venerable 5.0L pushrod small-block was traded for the thoroughly modern single-overhead-cam 4.6-liter V8. From there the Mustang continued galloping on into a new millennium and remains running strong as Ford celebrates its 100th birthday.

SPECIFICATIONS

Engine: 215-horsepower 5.0L (302 cubic inches) OHV V8

Bore & stroke: 4.00 x 3.00 inches

Compression: 9.0:1

Fuel delivery: sequential fuel injection

Transmission: five speed manual, standard; AOD automatic, optional

Steering: rack and pinion with power assist

Suspension: independent MacPherson strut, front; four-link setup with solid axle and coil springs, rear

Brakes: four-wheel discs

Price: $17,270, coupe; $21,960 convertible

Wheelbase: 101.3 inches

Weight: 3,258 pounds, coupe; 3,414 pounds, convertible

Model availability: two-door coupe and convertible

Construction: unitized body/frame

Production: 78,480 coupes (base V6 & GT); 44,713 convertibles (base V6 and GT)

1995 Mustang Cobra-R

The more things change, the more they stay the same. In 1965 Dearborn decision-makers wanted to see their newborn Mustang promoting the Blue Oval in sanctioned stock-class racing, so they looked west to Carroll Shelby in California. He transformed Ford's polite pony into the race-ready GT-350R, a mean machine that quickly put the Corvette guys in their place.

Nearly 30 years later, Ford execs again hoped to see their Mustang take a more prominent roll in production-class competition. This time it was Dearborn's newly formed Special Vehicle Team that stepped in, introducing its Cobra R Mustang in 1993. Based on the last of the Fox-chassis Mustangs, the 1993 SVT Cobra R coupe featured big disc brakes, a stiffened body pan borrowed from the Mustang convertible, and a suspension held up by big 17x8 wheels.

Of course these semi-civilized rough-riders were meant to go right to the track. After all, the "R" stood for "racing," not "run-to-the-store." Nonetheless, many of the 107 R-models built for 1993 ended up like museum pieces in collectors' garages. So SVT officials tried a different tack when they rolled out a second-edition R-model Mustang for 1995.

SVT announced the 1995 Cobra R in December 1994. Also mentioned was a small detail: the latest R-model would be sold by the 720 SVT dealers only to individuals "who could show evidence of current membership in a recognized sanctioning body, as well as additional proof of his intent to campaign the

car." There would be no collector/investor exploitation this time. Red tape aside, all 250 1995 Cobra R Mustangs were spoken for almost overnight after SVT started taking orders on January 5. It was then only a matter of months before new R-models started showing up for resale in classified ads with asking prices as high as $50,000. So much for best-laid plans.

Those lucky enough to have acquired one of those 250 cars was treated to the Mustang's Mustang, the potent ponycar enthusiasts had been begging for since the late-1980s. Beneath that bulging fiberglass hood was the famous 5.0L HO V8's bigger brother, the 351 cubic-inch Windsor small-block, the engine then being used in SVT's trick Lightning F150 pickup. With GT-40 heads and induction equipment, the Lightning's 5.8L V8 produced 240 horsepower. More cam and compression upped that ante to 300 horsepower for the Cobra R.

Since the 1995 Cobra R was not meant for everyday operation, all 250 examples were delivered in the same plain-Jane fashion: all came without a heater, radio or backseat, and all were painted white. No nonsense was clearly the intention for this rarin' to race Mustang. How many of them actually raced is a good question.

SPECIFICATIONS

Engine: *300-horsepower 351 cubic-inch Windsor small-block V8 with GT-40 cast-iron cylinder heads*

Bore & stroke: *4.00 x 3.50 inches*

Compression: *9.0:1*

Fuel delivery: *electronic-controlled sequential port fuel injection with two-piece GT-40 aluminum intake*

Exhaust: *tubular headers*

Fuel capacity: *20 gallons in racing-style fuel cell*

Transmission: *heavy-duty Tremec five-speed manual*

Suspension: *MacPherson strut up front, four-link setup with solid axle in back; heavy-duty springs, shocks and stabilizer bars*

Wheels: *17x9 cast-aluminum five-spokes with special "R" caps*

Tires: *B.F. Goodrich Comp T/A PR255/45ZR-17*

Price: *$35,499*

Wheelbase: *101.3 inches*

Length: *181.5 inches*

Weight: *3.326 pounds*

Model availability: *two-door coupe*

Construction: *unitized body/frame*

Production: *250, all painted white with no radio, heater or backseat*

1997 Ford F-150 Pickup Truck

Prior to the 1970s, it had been Chevy trucks in the sales lead for roughly 30 years straight. Then Ford turned the table on its arch-rival and has yet to look back while running up its own streak. Most pickup buyers today undoubtedly cannot even recall when Ford was not America's best-selling truck.

Still fresh in their memories, though, was a startling modernization made as the F-series truck was poised to celebrate its 50th anniversary on (and off) America's roads. Introduced with a lot of fuss and publicity in January 1996, the 1997 F-150 pickup left its boxy forerunners well behind thanks to an aerodynamic restyle which critics either loved or hated. There was almost no middle ground. Buyers, however, mostly fit into the former class as they clearly could not resist Ford's latest, greatest F-series truck. Demand immediately overwhelmed supply and continued doing so throughout 1996.

Additional attractions included the all-new "Triton" series modular engines, which traded traditional pushrods for cutting edge overhead-cam construction. First in the Triton lineup was a 4.2-liter V8, standard for all but Ford's 4x4 "Supercab" trucks. Optional were the 4.6- and 5.4-liter Triton V8s.

Four-wheel disc brakes were standard, too, for the first time in pickup history. The 1997 F-150 also marked a departure from Ford's almost legendary Twin I-Beam front suspension, a simple layout first marketed with great fanfare for 1965. New for 1997 was a modern "car-like" independent front suspension with parallel A-arms and torsion bars, an arrangement that markedly improved ride and handling.

Another milestone of sorts, the lengthened Supercab F-150 for 1997 featured the light-truck market's first "third door," which allowed passenger's easy access to the rear seating area from the pickup's curbside only. Chevrolet had introduced a third-door for its cabs in 1996, but it was an option that first year. Three-

door cabs soon became all the rage around Detroit once Ford made them standard issue. Next came full-sized four-door bodies as rivals continued the fight to overthrow the pickup market king.

Yet regardless of what they do, those imposters to the throne have yet to bring down America's number-one truck, long live F-150.

SPECIFICATIONS

Engine: 4.2-liter SOHC V6: 4.6 and 5.4-liter V8s optional

Fuel delivery: sequential multi-port electronic fuel injection with EEC-V electronic engine management

Transmission: five-speed overdrive manual transmission, standard; four-speed automatic overdrive transmission, optional

Suspension: independent control arms with torsion bars, front; longitudinal leaf springs and solid axle in back

Brakes: four-wheel discs with rear-wheel ABS

Price: $26,670 (for two-wheel-drive 5.4L V8 Flareside Supercab with Lariat trim)

Wheelbase: 139 inches

Weight: 4,200 pounds

Model availability: three-door SuperCab half-ton pickup truck with short Flareside cargo box; Lariat trim package, optional

Construction: body on frame, rear-wheel drive (four-wheel drive, optional); boxed-rail frame with six cross-members

Production: (all models on all chassis): 710,301

1998 Lincoln Navigator

On July 1, 1997, Lincoln set out on a journey to unfamiliar territory where no American luxury maker had gone before. Select Lincoln dealers that day unveiled the Navigator, America's latest and most prestigious sport-utility-vehicle. Following hot on the heels of Ford's other all-new SUVs, Mercury's Mountaineer and Ford's Expedition, the 1998 Navigator set out to prove that Ford could easily dominate a large sector of the sport-ute market. In 1990 the SUV population in America had been 900,000. The final tally for 1997 topped 2 million, and one out of every six vehicles on the road in 1998 was a sport-utility. So many companies had jumped into the market by then you almost needed a scorecard to tell the players apart. But leave it to Lincoln to make up its own rules.

"The evolution of the sport-utility market moves to the next higher level with the introduction of Navigator," said Jim O'Connor, Ford Motor Company vice president in charge of Lincoln. "Our customers will get the best of both worlds with Navigator. They will find the distinctive style and comfort of Lincoln along with the full capability and adventure of a premium full-size sport utility."

Luxury sport-utes were certainly nothing new in 1997, at least from a worldwide perspective. Lexus and Range Rover were then already out there and still positioned well above the niche Lincoln had carved for the Navigator, but that positioning was no accident. At the time, Range Rovers were running in the $55,000-65,000 range and Lexus' LX450 was bringing between $49,000 and $53,000. The new Navigator's base price was $39,950 for the two-wheel-drive and $43,300 for its more "rugged" 4x4.

With such a major price gap between America's first truly luxurious sport-utility and its overseas rivals, the Navigator at first traveled a course almost all to itself in the market, leaving the elitist, wannabe buyers to their wretched excesses. In the late-1990s, customers who tried to compare the domestic Lincoln with its high-brow import rivals were undoubtedly left wondering where all those extra thousands of dollars went.

Luxury, prestige and functionality were all there in spades from Lincoln, the Ford Expedition had emerged as a truly distinctive show-stopper. Leading the way up front was an obviously "Lincoln-esque" grille complemented by a unique lower fascia fitted with twin recessed foglamps. Standard running boards, conveniently illuminated, were both practical and stylish. Even the standard tow hitch in back was designed with an eye towards both form and function. Luxury treatments included leather appointments inside accented with burled

walnut on the dash and console. The steering wheel was also walnut, trimmed in leather. Being a Lincoln, the Navigator also came as quiet as an SUV then could—NVH (that is noise, vibration, harshness) suppression was of course key to the design, and the ride was also exceptionally non-SUV-like thanks to a standard air suspension and specially chosen shocks and tires. The Navigator still upheld its Lincoln heritage, even off the beaten path.

As for nuts and bolts, power came from Ford's big 5.4-liter V8 backed by a four-speed automatic transmission, the Control-Trac automatic four-wheel-drive system was optional to the basic deal. That standard Class III towing package could handle up to 8,000 pounds, while maximum payload capacity was 1,800 pounds, though it was unclear as to just how many buyers were actually interested in showing off the Navigator's truck side.

SPECIFICATIONS

Engine: 230-horsepower 5.4-liter EFI V8

Bore & stroke: 3.55 x 4.16 inches

Transmission: 4R1000 electronic four-speed automatic overdrive

Brakes: four-wheel anti-lock discs

Price: $39,950 for standard two-wheel-drive; $43,300 for four-wheel-drive

Wheelbase: 119 inches

Overall length: 204.8 inches

Cargo area: 116.4 cubic feet

Model availability: four-door sporty-utility vehicle

Fuel capacity: 30 gallons

Fuel economy (EPA estimated): 14/18 mpg city/highway for two-wheel-drive; 13/17 mpg city/highway for four-wheel-drive

1999 Mercury Cougar

Like its Thunderbird running mate from Ford, Mercury's Cougar was dropped in 1997 only to be reborn a short time later. Beating the latest, greatest T-bird out of the blocks by a couple years, a totally redesigned Cougar was first introduced to America in January 1998 at Detroit's North American International Auto Show. A complete break from tradition, the repackaged Cougar traded its humbly upscale, quasi-luxurious place in the market for a smaller, sportier, more affordable niche, itself an all-new segment for a division long known for its appeal to a gentler, older set.

That stoic group's diminishing impact in the marketplace, coupled with heavy competition from the ever-expanding sport-utility field, had forced Ford officials' hand concerning the Cougar's long-running story. By the late 1990s it had become time to turn the page to attract a totally new readership or close the book entirely. Indeed a rewrite of Mercury's cat tale involved a less age-challenged, more fad-conscious class, featuring Generation Xers finally coming of age and baby boomers still young enough to have open minds. Young women were also given their fair share of attention by a design crew whose task it was to chart a new course for Mercury.

The 1999 Cougar was clearly a different breed of feline, thanks most prominently to what Mercury execs prefer to call "New Edge Design," an approach obviously aimed at active drivers familiar with life in the fast lane.

"Just like the Navigator changed the way people think about Lincoln, Cougar [now] will make it cool to own a Mercury," said Lincoln-Mercury general manager Jim O'Connor in 1998. While the new Cougar remained a two-door coupe, its downsized stature and sharp-edged sexiness was intended to attract an equally new breed of buyer to a nameplate that first appeared in 1967 alongside the Mustang in Ford Motor Company's ponycar corral.

Still very much representative of Detroit stylists' love affair with the ellipse, the 1999 Cougar at the same time stood as an intriguing departure from typical trends. Slashing highlights created a sense of motion while standing still, and contrasting angular head- and taillight structures caught the eye with ease.

Beneath the skin was a platform made up mostly of proven, practical corporate hardware. About 70 per cent of Cougar components came from the existing Contour/Mystique parts bins. Yet even with these mundane technical ties, the 1999 Cougar was not just another "grocery-getter."

"The new Cougar is a stylish, sophisticated, mid-sized sports coupe that combines innovative design, exhilarating driving character and practicality all in one package," explained Will Boddie, Ford Motor

Company's Small and Medium Vehicle Center vice president.

Agility-conscious chassis tweaks and low-profile tires did indeed leave Cougar drivers with certainly sporty impressions. Even the exhaust note had a playful, performance-type tone. And with the optional 170-horsepower, 24-valve, 2.5-liter Duratec V6 installed, the new Cougar's voice went from purr to hiss without notice. Base power came from a 125-horse, 16-valve 2.0-liter Zetec four-cylinder.

An impressive list of additional standard features included air conditioning, 15-inch aluminum wheels, power windows and door locks, power height-adjustable driver's seat, rear defroster, tilt steering column and AM/FM stereo with cassette player. V6 Cougars got 16-inch wheels and ABS, while anti-lock brakes were optional for Zetec-equipped Cougars. Safety-enhancing side airbags—a first for Ford on this side of the Atlantic—also were listed as a $375 Cougar option. Base sticker for the 1999 Cougar was $16,595. Throwing in two more cylinders put the price at $18,495. Exchanging the five-speed for the automatic transaxle boosted the bottom line up to $19,310.

Production of the next-generation Cougar began at

SPECIFICATIONS

Engine: *125-horse, 2.0-liter Zetec four-cylinder standard; 170-horse 2.5-liter Duratec V6 optional*

Bore & stroke: *3.34 x 3.46 inches for Zetec four; 3.24 x 3.13 inches for Duratec six*

Transmission: *MTX75 five-speed manual overdrive standard; CD4E four-speed automatic transmission optional*

Price: *$16,595 for base four-cylinder; $18,495 for optional V6*

Wheelbase: *106.5 inches*

Weight: *2,900 pounds*

Model availability: *two-door coupe*

Performance: *four-cylinder/manual trans; 0-60 mph in 10.5 seconds Four-cylinder/auto trans; 0-60 mph in 12.8 seconds V6/manual trans; 0-60 mph in 8.0 seconds V6/auto trans; 0-60 mph in 10.1 seconds*

Ford Motor Company's joint-venture (with Mazda) AutoAlliance International assembly plant in Flat Rock, Michigan, on March 16, 1998. Mercury's entry into the race for the next millennium then officially went on sale in May that year.

1999 Anniversary Mustang GT convertible

Ford never has been all that big on giving anniversary gifts, certainly not to the degree noticed around General Motors in recent decades. Special-edition commemorative Corvettes, Camaros and Firebirds were seemingly everywhere before the turn of the millennium. An exciting, all-new Mustang appeared for 1994 just in time to mark 30 years on the road for America's original ponycar, and what did Dearborn's proud product planners do? Other than let rumors fly, they did nothing. Not even a simple anniversary badge was slapped onto the 1994 Mustang.

And, no, those special-edition "7-UP green" models did not quite fill the bill back in 1990. The badge used on that one even stated "25 Years," which did not quite add up—the Mustang was born in 1964, not 1965.

At least Ford vice president (and Ford Division president) Jim O'Connor got the math right when he introduced the restyled 1999 Mustang. "The Mustang was introduced 35 years ago next April, and the car always has projected an attitude that is free-spirited, fun and definitely cool," he said in October 1998. It was that long-running cool attitude, combined with a new, fresh feel, that O'Connor's design team were hoping to capture when taking the next step ahead into the ponycar's future.

"[The 1999] design is strong, contemporary and true to Mustang's original concept," said

chief program engineer Janine Bay. Indeed, the 1999 Mustang offered the best of both worlds to the devoted ponycar rider. At the same time it was "something old, something new."

The product of Ford's "New Edge" design school, the 1999 Mustang followed similarly in the taut tracks of the angular, aggressive GT-90 concept car shown off a few years before. Chiseled lines and sharp creases replaced the soft contours and compound curves that, according to some critics, allowed the previous ponycar body to look very "Japanese," an impression that Ford people claimed they had tried to avoid at all costs.

But along with all those contemporary exterior touches, Gaffka's designers also did everything they could to remind customers of the Mustang's 35-year heritage. On the front was the traditional galloping pony, now circled by a chrome "corral" in a honeycomb grille just as it was in 1964. Traditional sculptured side scoops behind the doors and tri-bar taillights also stirred memories, as did the scooped muscular hood.

Improvements beneath the skin included considerably more horsepower for both the base V6 and the GT's 4.6L SOHC V8. Chassis upgrades further improved ride, handling and steering, and revised floorpan sealing reduced road noise. Convertible platforms were also reinforced to get a better handle on inherent body shakes.

And, oh yes, the new Mustang for 1999 did finally mark a major anniversary, something not seen to this degree in the ponycar corral since 1984. All 1999 models were treated to "35th-Anniversary" fender badges and specially embossed commemorative bucket seats. No, it was not much. But it was better than nothing.

SPECIFICATIONS

Engine: 260-horsepower 4.6L SOHC V8

Bore & stroke: 3.6 x 3.6 inches

Compression: 9.0:1

Fuel delivery: sequential electronic fuel injection

Transmission: five-speed manual, standard; four-speed electronic automatic overdrive, optional

Suspension: MacPherson struts up front; four-link system with coil springs and solid axle in back

Steering: power-assisted rack and pinion

Brakes: power-assisted four-wheel discs; ABS optional

Wheels: 16x7.5 forged aluminum, standard; 17x8 forged aluminum, optional

Tires: P225/55HR16 B.F. Goodrich, standard; P245/45ZR17 Goodyear Eagle, optional

Price: $29,360

Wheelbase: 101.3 inches

Length: 183.2 inches

Height: 53.3 inches

Weight: 3,386 pounds

Model availability: two-door convertible (GT Mustang also offered as coupe)

Construction: unitized body/frame

2000 Ford Focus Sony Edition

Ford's latest attempt at building a "world car" came in 2000 in the form of the attractive Focus, an almost amazingly roomy compact that showcased the company's "New Edge" design approach in its cutest form. With its tall "greenhouse" and sharp corners, the Focus body seemingly looked bigger from the inside than from out. Headroom especially benefited from all that angularity, but it was not lacking in legroom either, at least not for a 2500-pound mini-machine rolling on a 103-inch wheelbase.

Standard power came from a 2.0-liter Zetec four-cylinder that was both reasonably peppy and frugal to the bone. This 110-horse four was rated at 33 mpg on the highway, 25 around town. Those numbers dropped, of course, if the optional 130-horsepower 2.0-liter was ordered. Along with this engine came a rear spoiler and a tachometer in what was called the "sport group."

Typically defeating the budget-conscious purpose as well, were options like power windows, ABS brakes, side-impact airbags and the "comfort group" with its tilt steering column and speed control. Far and away the

most expensive option, at $1,595, was the Sony package, which included a Sony stereo, a leather-wrapped steering wheel and 15-inch alloy wheels. Sony custom-designed the Xplod sound system for the Sony Limited Edition Ford Focus, carefully matching the placement of the components to optimize the acoustics. The speaker size and power output combo is rated by Ford publicity as "ideal for those who want to emulate the quality of their home systems in their cars." All told, a fully loaded Sony-edition 2000 Focus with the 130-horse sport group ran up around $17,500—not a bad price, but a bit more than many compact buyers around the world care to stomach.

SPECIFICATIONS

Engine: 110-horsepower 2.0-liter inline four-cylinder

Fuel delivery: sequential electronically controlled fuel injection

Transmission: five-speed manual transaxle

Steering: rack and pinion with power assist

Suspension: independent MacPherson struts and coils springs, front; multi-link with coil springs, rear

Brakes: front discs, rear drums (ABS optional)

Price: $13,565, base (Sony package cost $1,595 extra)

Wheelbase: 103 inches

Weight: 2,552 pounds

Model availability: two-door hatchback coupe, four-door sedan and station wagon

Construction: unitized body/frame with front-wheel drive

2001-03: Into the New Millennium

"The competition can build cars, but they can't win customers' hearts the way Mustang and Thunderbird have. We intend to leverage that advantage by rolling out new versions of our current legends and gauge the market's appetite for other historically significant automobiles."

ABOVE: *The banner says it all. The Taurus model series had appeared in the U.S. in 1986, selling close on a quarter of a million in the first year of production.*

By most counts, the big day will come on June 16, 2003, the date that Ford Motor Company officially turns 100 years old. But for many of the Ford faithful, the celebration had actually begun nearly two years before, in October 2001. One-hundred years prior to that point in time, Henry Ford had beaten Alexander Winton in a race at Grosse Pointe, Michigan, an event that vaulted the Ford name into the limelight and thus supplied young Henry with the momentum (as well as investment capital) he needed to eventually open his own car company. Of course, it took him three tries to get it right, but once he did there was no stopping Ford from becoming the world's most renowned automotive nameplate.

Ford officials marked this magic moment at the track with another special event, this one held October 13-14, 2001, at Dearborn's Greenfield Village. On hand were about 200 historic racing cars, joined by more than few equally historic drivers, such as Dan Gurney, Parnelli Jones, Junior Johnson, Don Nicholson, and Lyn St. James. Also on hand was the restored "Sweepstakes" car Henry had driven to victory in 1901. Another running replica of that racer, with Edsel Ford II driving, was paired off against a replica of Winton's machine, driven by Winton heir Charles Wake. True to form, the Ford won again.

It was a grand celebration of one of automotive history's greatest competitive legacies, which explains why Dearborn officials spared little expense throwing the party. "More than any other manufacturer in the world, Ford has both defined and differentiated itself in the marketplace by taking advantage of the opportunities presented by racing," said Bob Rewey, group vice president of marketing sales and service. "We can't overstate the importance of racing to our business." Ford additionally cannot overstate the significance of its 100th anniversary, explaining why an even greater party is scheduled for June 12-16, 2003, at Dearborn's Henry Ford II World Center. Ford racers will again be honored at this event, but so too will all the various products that have rolled off the Ford assembly line since 1903. Without a doubt the nostalgia will be as thick as molasses; century-old molasses, that is.

But that is the way many minds at Ford prefer it today. Planning well ahead for the future is of course the top priority around Dearborn these days, but of notable importance too is a desire to remind buyers what the Ford brand name has meant to so many people for so many years now. Along with building America's best-selling light trucks and SUVs, Ford has also teased us with an intriguing lineup of too-cool-for-school concept cars, of which some have already almost amazingly found their way from auto show stages into regular production. Most prominent is the new two-seat Thunderbird, a car that captures the imagination as easily as its tantalizing first-generation forerunners of 1955-57. And by the time you read this, work will be

RIGHT: *The retro-styled Thunderbird, first marketed in 2000, shares a platform with the Jaguar S-Type and the Lincoln LS.*

BELOW: *Attention to detail is what separates the elegant 2002 Lincoln Blackwood from run-of-the-mill pick-ups. The luxury car maker entered the 4x4 field with the fabulous Navigator and shows no sign of compromising at any level.*

finishing on the totally awesome GT40, a veritable reincarnation of the racing machine that beat the world four years running in France from 1966 to 1969.

"We're extremely fortunate to have a heritage at Ford that is unmatched in the industry," said J. Mays, Ford's vice president of design and the driving force behind the company's "Living Legends" Design Studio. "The competition can build cars, but they can't win customers' hearts the way Mustang and Thunderbird have. We intend to leverage that advantage by rolling out new versions of our current legends and gauge the market's appetite for other historically significant automobiles."

Located in two buildings on Ford's Product Development campus in Dearborn, the Living Legends studio is where Mays and studio director Doug Gaffka's staff have made recent history. Creating the studio just sort of happened in 2001, according to Mays. "One day, we were just talking about how fortunate we are to have 'powerbrands' like Thunderbird and Mustang in our portfolio and we characterized them as 'Living Legends," he said. "The phrase caught on."

Hot on the heels of the first "Living Legend," the 1999 Thunderbird concept car, came the next, the 2001 "Forty-Nine." Inspired by the redesigned 1949 Ford, the car that had helped Henry Ford II turn things around a half century back, the Forty-Nine concept car, in Ford's words, "harkens back to the romance of a Friday night at the drive-in or bowling ally, listening to rock-and-roll and cruising 'the strip' in a chopped and

"One day, we were just talking about how fortunate we are to have 'powerbrands' like Thunderbird and Mustang in our portfolio and we characterized them as 'Living Legends,'" he said. "The phrase caught on."

BELOW: *The return of the Glory Days. A GT40 Replica—a true "Living Legend"—prepares to launch itself into the far, blue yonder. Henry Ford would be well pleased...*

channeled custom car." Smooth as silk is a fair description for this dream machine, which officials have hinted might also make its way onto Mainstreet U.S.A.

Mays and crew followed that flight of fancy up with the edgy "Ford 427" in 2003, chosen by *AutoWeek* editors as that year's Best Concept car at Detroit's annual North American International Auto Show. Based on a lengthened Lincoln LS platform, the boxy, brawny 427 was created to help revive recollections of Ford's Total Performance years, a time when men were men, women were not and a pack of Camels rolled up in a T-shirt sleeve was the only fashion statement you needed. "With 590 horses on tap, the 427's V10 not only rekindles memories of the big and bad sedan's heyday of the Sixties, it shows Ford is serious about putting power and performance back into its mainstay vehicles," claimed *AutoWeek*.

Mays is also serious about the legendary Mustang, which continues galloping along after its ponycar rivals from Chevrolet and Pontiac were cancelled two years back. Word of the next-generation Mustang, an aggressive, downright intimidating rendition that will combine familiar cues with a truly futuristic feel, had already leaked out late in 2002. Plans are for the car to appear in the fall of 2004 as a 2005 model, but those who have seen mock-ups and concepts already can't wait.

We can only wonder what Ford has in store for us over the next hundred years.

2001 Ford SVT Lightning F-150

Ford's Special Vehicle Team has been responsible for some of Detroit's hottest factory hot rods dating back to its first Mustang Cobra in 1993. But do not think for a minute that the SVT's focus has been limited to cars alone. Also introduced in 1993 was the Lightning pickup truck, a half-ton hauler powered by a 240-horse 351 V8.

As for the F-150 Lightning, it temporarily faded from the scene that year, though not for long. When it returned for 1999, it was fitted with a supercharged 351 that pumped out 360 horsepower, enough muscle to propel the second-generation SVT pickup from 0-60 in 6.2 seconds—sensational performance considering the truck weighed nearly two-and-a-half tons. Sales for the "blown" Lightning, however, were not so hot as only 8,966 left SVT dealerships in 1999 and 2000 combined.

But Ford would not give up easily. New wheels and a revamped front fascia were

not the only things setting the 2001 SVT Lightning apart. Behind that aggressive-looking snout were 20 more horses, delivered to the road via shorter rear gears: 3.73:1 compared to 3.55:1. That Roots-type Eaton blower remained in place atop the 2001 Lightning's 351 V8, but it worked in concert with a few enlarged pieces (mass airflow meter and air intake opening) and a higher-flow intake manifold.

The new 380-horsepower output figure not only looked impressive on paper, it also amounted to some serious performance gains. Reportedly it covered 0-60 in only 5.8 seconds, while the quarter-mile went by in 13.9 clicks. Top end was listed at 142 mph—and remember, we are still talking about a pickup truck here. Yes, but this pickup wore an SVT badge, and those three letters said it all.

SPECIFICATIONS

Engine: *380-horsepower 5.4-liter Triton SOHC V8 with aluminium cylinder heads*

Compression: *8.4:1*

Fuel delivery: *sequential electronic fuel injection with Eaton supercharger and water-to-air intercooler*

Transmission: *four-speed 4R100 automatic*

Brakes: *four-wheel discs with power assist and ABS*

Steering: *re-circulating ball with power assist*

Suspension: *short/long control arms with coil springs, front and Bilstein shock absorbers, front; longitudinal, leaf springs with solid axle and staggered Bilstein shock absorbers, rear*

Price: *$32,460*

Wheelbase: *119.8*

Weight: *4,670 pounds*

Model availability: *two-door half-ton pickup truck*

Construction: *body on frame*

2001 Bullitt Mustang

Many consider it to be one of the greatest car-chase scenes in Hollywood history: Steve McQueen in his dark green Mustang tailing that sinister Dodge Charger up, over and around the streets of San Francisco. The sounds, the fury, the fiery explosion at the end—could it get any better? As classic movies go, McQueen's 1968 film *Bullitt* may rank well down the list, but those 12-odd minutes of squealing tires and gutsy exhaust notes will never be forgotten, especially by enthusiasts who just cannot seem to get enough of anything involving a Mustang.

So at a time when nostalgia seems to be the hot ticket around Dearborn,

why not revive a bit of that old Bullitt magic? That is what project manager Scott Hoag's team did when they put together the special-edition Bullitt Mustang. First shown in concept car form at the Los Angeles Auto Show in January 2000, the 2001 Bullitt Mustang went on sale in April 2001 to the delight of fans of both the car and the movie.

Like the two 1968 fastbacks specially prepared for McQueen 35 years ago, the latter-day Bullitt Mustang received various suspension tweaks to allow it to chase after anything on four wheels on demand. Stiffer springs and shocks, thicker anti-roll bars and stiffening subframe connectors were also joined by bigger brakes to better handle an encore performance of that 1968 scene. Only this time the driver could also rely on ABS and traction control to hopefully avoid a ditch like the one McQueen ended up in. Five more horses beneath the

hood resulted from, among other things, a specially tuned exhaust system that gave the Bullitt Mustang a growl reminiscent of the rumblings that helped the movie *Bullitt* draw an Academy Award nomination for sound. Also mimicking McQueen's ride were the American Racing wheels chosen for the Bullitt Mustang.

Additional special touches included a racing-type brushed aluminum gas filler door, red brake calipers and "Bullitt" block letters on the tail. Retro-style instrumentation and upholstery, extra brightwork for the shifter and floor pedals, and exclusive door sills further dramatized the image.

All that remained was for a Bullitt Mustang driver to prove that he or she could hit those switchbacks better than McQueen.

SPECIFICATIONS

Engine: *265-horsepower 4.6-liter SOHC V8*

Bore & stroke: *3.55 x 3.54 inches*

Transmission: *five-speed manual*

Steering: *rack and pinion with power assist*

Suspension: *independent MacPherson struts with coil springs, front; independent with control arms, toe-control links and coil springs, rear*

Brakes: *four-wheel discs with power assist*

Price: *$26,830*

Wheelbase: *101.3 inches*

Weight: *3,273 pounds*

Model availability: *two-door coupe*

Construction: *unitized body/frame*

2002 Ford Thunderbird

There was a reason why Ford officials chose not to publicize the Thunderbird's farewell in 1997: it was not final. Almost everyone knew the badge would be back, but in what form? Would Dearborn designers honor an automotive legend or simply play off it for promotional sake?

Answers to all questions came in January 1999 when Ford chief Jacques Nasser and design exec J Mays unveiled a curious yellow concept car at the North American International Auto Show in Detroit. Though the nameplate clearly read "Thunderbird," show-goers all surely identified the cute, little convertible without any introductions, thanks to more than one familiar facet. Nearly 45 years after it

had sadly went away, the classic two-seat T-bird would come back for 2002, promised Mays, and it would bring along with it many fond memories. "The all-new Thunderbird is designed to point to the future while recapturing the magic of an

American icon," he said. "[t]here are only a select few nameplates that have earned their way into the hearts of the motoring public by establishing a true heritage. Thunderbird is certainly one of them."

While nostalgic styling cues were obvious inside and out, the 2002 Thunderbird still could claim an identity all its own, thanks primarily to the wonders of modern technology. Computer-aided design work produced a super-rigid chassis that helped a car that looks so small feel so big. The new 'Bird's comfortable, sure ride on its own helped leave the past behind, as did anti-lock disc brakes at the corners and a nicely powerful 3.9-liter dual-overhead-cam V8 beneath that scooped hood. Zero to 60 mph in about 7 seconds was a breeze—try squeezing that kind of performance out of a 1957 T-bird.

But if remaining lost in the 1950s is still your bag, the latest, greatest Thunderbird's optional hardtop does require two people to lift on or off, although the modern-day rendition is a bit lighter, a lot quicker to attach/detach, and comes with a convenient cart for safe keeping when off.

Either way, with hardtop in place or skin to the wind, today's T-bird driver faces a fun ride ahead. Or behind, depending on how you look at things.

SPECIFICATIONS

Engine: 252-horsepower 3.9-liter 32-valve DOHC V8

Bore & stroke: 3.44 x 2.4 inches

Compression: 10.55:1

Fuel delivery: sequential multi-port electronic fuel injection

Transmission: five-speed automatic overdrive

Brakes: four-wheel discs with power assist and ABS

Steering: variable-assist rack and pinion

Suspension: independent short/long control arms with coil springs, front; independent short/long arm with coil springs

Price: $35,495

Wheelbase: 107.2 inches

Length: 186.3 inches

Height: 52.1 inches

Weight: 3,775 pounds

Model availability: two-door convertible

Construction: unitized body/frame with three stiffening X-braces

2002 Lincoln Blackwood pickup truck

Okay, so maybe nobody actually asked for a luxury pickup. Nonetheless, both Cadillac and Lincoln have produced such machines, if only to keep Texas oil tycoons riding in high style while surveying all that they master.

Lincoln's Blackwood, introduced for a brief run in 2002, could have served few other purposes. It was rigged to tow 8,700 pounds, so transporting your thoroughbred to the Kentucky Derby was a possibility, as well as a consideration that was no coincidence. J. Mays' designers surely targeted the mint julep set with this posh pickup, and that helps explain why they did not bother to specify four-wheel-drive equipment for the Blackwood like engineers had previously done for the Navigator sport-ute. Who needs to go off-road to get to the country club anyway?

Basically a stretched Navigator with a custom "cargo trunk" (Lincoln's words) added on in back, the Blackwood had debuted along with the new T-bird at the Detroit Auto Show in 1999. Apparently oohs and aahs were enough to convince Lincoln planners to produce a limited run of a limited utility vehicle that favored form over function many times over. And once Blackwood production was announced

Cadillac's creative crowd could not help but counter with their Escalade, every bit as much as a prima donna pickup as the Lincoln.

Calling the Blackwood a truck was, at best, a reach. Though there was 26.5 cubic feet of usable space behind those convenient "Dutch doors" in back, no way a washer and/or dryer would ever find their way onto the Blackwood's freight list. First, that power-operated hard tonneau cover did not come off. Second, a carpeted floor and stainless steel inner panels (with LED accent lighting)

host of standard accoutrements completed the Blackwood package, which sold for nearly $52,000 in 2002. The only option was a $2,000 navigation system—a feature that surely came in handy while traversing a Texas ranch as big as Connecticut.

clearly beckoned only to more precious cargo—like golf clubs or more gold clubs.

Simulated wood paneling around that cargo trunk's exterior, leather appointments inside, and a whole

SPECIFICATIONS

Engine: 300-horsepower 5.4-liter 32-valve DOHC V8

Bore & stroke: 3.55 x 4.17 inches

Compression: 9.5:1

Fuel delivery: electronic fuel injection

Transmission: four-speed automatic

Brakes: four-wheel discs with ABS

Steering: re-circulating ball with power assist

Suspension: independent short/long control arms with coil springs, front; longitudinal leaf springs with solid axle and trailing arms, rear

Price: $51,785

Wheelbase: 138.5

Length: 220.2

Height: 73.6 inches

Weight: 5,637 pounds

Model availability: four-door half-ton pickup truck

Construction: body on frame

2003 Mercury Marauder

One of the first questions Bill Ford asked after taking over as Ford Motor Company CEO in 2000 undoubtedly went something like, "what the hell is going on at Mercury?" Who was being targeted? Old? Young? Well-off? Not-so-well-off? By the looks of the division's products—ranging from the twenty-something-female-friendly Cougar to the get-the-grandparents-around-Florida Grand Marquis—not even Lincoln Mercury people themselves knew what direction they were heading. So William Clay Jr. laid down the law: find a distinctive identity or find work elsewhere.

Under the direction of 40-year-old Darrel Behmer, Mercury's first ever dedicated design chief, the Winged Messenger team wasted little time shifting gears, and it looks like not-so-good news for the blue-hair set. Rumors of an attitude change had already started making the rounds in 1998 after Steve Babcock's concept car creative group had rolled

out their 300-horsepower Marauder musclecar that year at the SEMA show in Las Vegas. That bad, black sedan was then joined on the 2002 auto show circuit by a Marauder convertible, a sexy supercharged cruiser clearly meant to get the blood pumping within arteries yet to be clogged by years of cholesterol abuse.

"The Marauder and the Marauder convertible concept say a lot about the next generation of Mercury vehicles, which we're defining now," explained Lincoln Mercury president Brian Kelley in 2002. "Both Marauders have heritage,

performance and charisma. You'll see these same qualities in future Mercurys."

While the Marauder convertible, with its 335-horse blown V8, remains a concept car at this moment, the Marauder sedan went into production in the summer of 2002, signaling that the future had indeed arrived at Mercury. Named after another class of powerful Mercurys first introduced in 1963, the 2003 Marauder sedan instantly reminded curbside kibitzers of Chevrolet's Impala SS of 1994-96, a family car that also served double-duty as a hot rod.

Like the first Impala SS, the new Marauder is only available in black, purposeful paint that contrasts its big 18-inch wheels, as well as those two bright exhaust tips in back. Supplying the serious sounds coming from those tips is an all-aluminum 4.6-liter 32-valve DOHC V8 that is more than capable of waking up the neighbors, even the ones that are not in bed by 8:00 pm. There's 302 horses hiding behind that blacked-out fascia and they are backed up by a beefy four-speed automatic transmission and 3.55:1 limited-slip gears. Road-worthy rack and pinion steering and big four-wheel disc brakes are also included in the deal.

Moving and shaking was once Mercury's thing back when the first Marauders roamed the earth. Now it looks like the company's future hinges on living a little in the past.

SPECIFICATIONS

Engine: 302-horsepower 4.6-liter DOHC V8 with four valves per cylinder

Bore & stroke: 3.6 x 3.6 inches

Compression: 10.1:1

Fuel delivery: Sequential multi-port electronic fuel injection

Transmission: four-speed automatic with overdrive

Brakes: hydraulic four-wheel discs; 11.1-inch rotors with single-piston calipers in back, 12.4-inch rotors with twin-piston calipers in front

Steering: speed-sensitive rack and pinion with variable power assist

Suspension: independent unequal A-arms with coil springs and a stabilizer bar in front; four-bar link with Watt's linkage, air springs, solid axle and stabilizer bar in back

Wheels: 18x8 aluminum-alloy five spoke

Tires: B.F. Goodrich g-Force T/A measuring P235/50WR18 in front, P245/55WR18 in back

Price: $34,495

Wheelbase: 114.7 inches

Length: 211.9 inches

Height: 56.8 inches

Weight: 4,165 pounds

Model availability: four-door five-passenger sedan

Construction: body on frame

2003 Ford GT40

What a way to celebrate a century in business. Taking dream cars off the auto show stage and putting them into production had become a relatively common practice these days, but William Clay Ford Jr. will undoubtedly take the cake in 2003 when he sets the reincarnated GT40 loose on Mainstreet U.S.A. to help mark his company's 100th anniversary. Easily as sleek and nearly as low as Ford's famous race cars of the 1960s—the "40" came from the car's height in inches—this outrageous two-seater should easily unseat Dodge's Viper as America's leading (make that only) "exoticar."

First shown off at the North American International Auto Show in Detroit in January 2002, the GT40 is a product of Doug Gaffka's Living Legends design studio. "It is the ultimate living legend," said Ford design exec J. Mays. "[It] is a true supercar with appeal equal to that of the greatest sports cars in the world, but with the addition of a heritage no one can match. It's the car that put Ford on the map in terms of international racing, and it signaled to the world that the Ford family doesn't settle for the status quo."

Ford followers old enough to have experienced the Total Performance years of the 1960s might recall reading about the original GT40's triumphant victory at Le Mans in 1966, a first for an American machine. Three more 24 Hours wins followed in 1967, 1968 and 1969 before Henry Ford II gave up on racing, but only after he had showed Enzo Ferrari what for.

Now Walter Mitty types will be able to relive those glory days in a civilized yet still super strong, thoroughly modernized version of the 200-mph racer that ruled the world 35 years back. That is as long as Mr. Mitty has $100,000 to blow on a car packed with 500 horses and few creature comforts.

"Like its namesake, the GT40 is not overwrought with advanced technologies," added Mays. "While it represents the best of Ford design, engineering and expertise, it is a no-frills machine. You won't find voice-

activated telematics here—not even power windows—just pure, refined performance."

John Coletti's SVT engineers created the GT40's supercharged 5.4-liter "Mod" motor, as well as the unique aluminum space frame consisting of a central cabin section, a front suspension sub-assembly and a powertrain cradle in back, all bolted together with utmost rigidity. On top of that solid

structure goes carbon-fiber body panels lovingly sculptured by Camilo Pardo, who spent many hours studying the original GT40, both on film and up close and personal. A vintage Ford racer was a fixture around the Living Legends studio during development work.

Bill Ford probably knew all along that the GT40 would become a production reality, but the showgoing public just had to be strung along for a month or so after the concept car's Detroit debut. Mr. Ford then made things official in February 2002.

Got your hundred-grand ready?

SPECIFICATIONS

Engine: 500-horsepower 5.4-liter DOHC 32-valve all-aluminum V8

Bore & stroke: 3.55 x 4.17 inches

Compression: 8.5:1

Fuel delivery: electronic fuel injection with supercharger and intercooler

Transmission: Tremec RBT six-speed transaxle

Brakes: Alcon four-wheel discs with six-piston calipers

Suspension: independent unequal-length control arms with pushrod/bellcrank system tied to horizontal spring dampers, front and rear

Wheels: 18x8, front; 19x10, rear

Tires: 245/45R18, front; 285/45R19, rear

Price (estimated): $100,000

Wheelbase: 106.7 inches

Length: 181.6 inches

Height: 43.5 inches

Weight: 3,000 pounds

Model availability: two-passenger, two-door mid-engined coupe

Construction: aluminum spaceframe with mid-mounted engine and rear-wheel drive; unstressed composite body

Production: projected at 1,000 annually

1894	1895	1896	1897	1898	1899	1900	1901	1902	1903	190

1896 Henry Ford drives his Quadricycle on the streets of Detroit. First moving pictures shown on a public screen in America.

1899 Henry Ford secures funding and opens the Detroit Automobile Company. Isthmian Canal Commission created to explore plans for a canal across Central America linking Atlantic and Pacific Oceans.

1901 Detroit Automobile Company dissolved. Henry Ford Company established. Henry Ford drives his first race car to victory against noted automaker Alexander Winton.

1904 Ford Motor Company of Canada founded. First sectio New York City subw system opened. Firs Olympics held in U. open in St. Louis, Missouri.

1903 Ford Motor Company founded in Detroit. Wright Brothers make first powered flight at Kitty Hawk, North Carolina. Boston Red Sox win Major League Baseball's first World Series. Barney Oldfield drives "999" race car to record speed of 64.5 mph.

1896 Quadricycle

BELOW: HENRY Ford at the helm of the 1896 Quadricycle.

1897 First Boston Marathon run. Famed Astoria Hotel opens in New York City.

1900 Eastman Kodak Company introduces its Brownie Box Camera.

1898 American battleship Maine blows up in Havana, Cuba, harbor. U.S. land and sea forces overwhelm Spanish counterparts in trumped-up Spanish-American War. Henry Ford builds his second Quadricycle.

1902 Cadillac Automobile Company formed from remnants of Henry Ford Company after Henry Ford resigns and takes name with him.

ABOVE: *Old 999, Ford's record-breaking, 1903 racer.*

Ford

| 1905 | 1906 | 1907 | 1908 | 1909 | 1910 | 1911 | 1912 | 1913 | 1914 | 1915 |

1905 Ford moves into larger plant on Piquette Avenue in Detroit. Number of automobiles registered in U.S. "soars" to nearly 79,000.

1910 Barney Oldfield ups world land speed record to 133 mph—this time driving a Benz. At Hampton Roads, Virginia, Eugene Ely flies first aircraft from the deck of a warship. Ford opens massive Highland Park plant in Detroit suburb.

1913 Ford begins selling Model Ts in the Far East. Moving assembly line goes into operation at Ford's Highland Park plant.

1911 Ford opens first branch assembly plant in Kansas City, Missouri; first overseas assembly plant opens near Manchester, England. First Memorial Day race run at Indianapolis.

1914 John and Horace Dodge, suppliers of Ford powertrains, open their own car company, Dodge Brothers. Henry Ford announces earth-shaking $5 workday for his plant employees. Black becomes sole color choice for Model T customers as production begins moving too fast to allow paints of the day to dry properly.

1907 Model K

1906 Ford share of the American automotive market jumps to 26 per cent. Henry Ford becomes president of company that bears his name. Major earthquake strikes San Francisco.

1908 Model T introduced. Early assembly line experiments begin at Piquette Avenue plant. Ford's first overseas sales branch opens in Paris.

1915 Ford's market share hits whopping 56 per cent. Henry Ford begins experiments with prototype tractors and buys land along Rouge River to build new plant. Booker T. Washington dies. German submarine torpedoes *Lusitania* off Ireland, killing 1,200 people and inspiring America's eventual entry into World War I.

RIGHT: *1911 Model T Torpedo Runabout*

1907 Famous advertising slogan, "Watch the Fords Go By," is penned. Lusitania, the world's largest ocean liner, arrives in New York after its maiden voyage from England.

1909 Mints in Philadelphia and San Francisco coin first Lincoln cent. U.S. population hits 92 million.

1912 S.S. *Titanic* hits iceberg and sinks in north Atlantic. Arizona, the 48th state, is admitted to the union. William Durant founds Chevrolet Motor Car Company.

1916   **1917**   **1918**   **1919**   **1920**   **1921**   **1922**   **1923**   **1924**   **1925**   **1926**

1916 Ford's first Latin-American assembly plant opened in Buenos Aires, Argentina. Total U.S. car and truck production surpasses one million mark for the first time.

1919 Henry Ford resigns company presidency; son Edsel Ford takes his place. Benson Ford born to Edsel and Eleanor. Henry Ford buys out all stockholders.

1922 Henry Ford buys Lincoln Motor Company for $8 million. Lincoln Memorial dedicated in Washington, D.C.

1925 Ford introduces first factory-complete, steel-bodied pickup truck. Henry Ford's third grandson, William Clay Ford, born. Ford of Japan formed in Yokohama.

1918 World War I ends. Chevrolet introduces its first trucks in both half- and one-ton forms—the latter is named Model T. Influenza epidemic kills nearly 500,000 people in America.

1924 10 millionth Model T built. George Gershwin's *Rhapsody in Blue* performed on piano for first time by Gershwin himself. Walter Chrysler begins building cars.

1917 America enters Great War in Europe. Ford introduces its first truck, the Model TT one-ton chassis. Dodge Brothers introduces its first truck for civilian sale. Henry Ford II born to Edsel and Eleanor Ford.

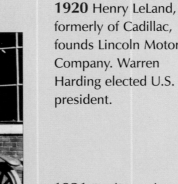

1919 "self-starting" Model T coupe.

1920 Henry LeLand, formerly of Cadillac, founds Lincoln Motor Company. Warren Harding elected U.S. president.

1923 Col. Jacob Shick patents first electric shaver.

1926 Colors oth black offered aga Model T. Ford be assembling Mod Germany.

1921 Ford's market share reaches new high of 61.5 per cent. William S. Knudsen quits Ford; later joins Chevrolet.

1927 | **1928** | **1929** | **1930** | **1931** | **1932** | **1933** | **1934** | **1935** | **1936** | **1937**

LEFT: *1925 Model T pickup*

1933 Franklin Roosevelt inaugurated for first of four U.S. presidential terms.

1936 Author Margaret Mitchell publishes *Gone With The Wind.*

BELOW: *1933 Lincoln Model KB*

1927 Last Model T built. Chevrolet takes over sales lead from Ford.

1929 Model A production reaches one million and two million mark. Stock market crashes in November. Richard Byrd makes first flight over South Pole.

1930 Astronomers discover ninth planet, Pluto.

1931 Empire State becomes World's tallest building

1934 Outlaws Clyde Barrow (of Bonnie & Clyde fame) and John Dillinger both write Henry Ford in praise of his automobiles, which neither men actually purchased themselves.

1932 Henry Ford introduces his "eight for the price of four," America's first affordable, mass-produced V8 engine.

1935 Publisher William Randolph Hearst earns America's largest salary; actress Mae West claims second largest.

ABOVE: *1928 Model A Tudor two-door sedan*

1928 New Model A Ford debuts to rave reviews. Walter Chrysler buys Dodge Brothers and introduces Plymouth and De Soto lines.

1931 Ford builds 20 millionth vehicle. Henry Ford lays off 75,000 workers due to depressed economy.

1937 Harry Bennett's "Service Department" henchman clash with union wworkers in "Battle of the Overpass" outside Ford works.

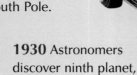

1938   **1939**   **1940**   **1941**   **1942**   **1943**   **1944**   **1945**   **1946**   **1947**   **194**

RIGHT: *Ford engined "Jeep" from 1943.*

1945 Both Germany and Japan surrender. Henry Ford finally resigns and Henry Ford II takes over as president. Harry Bennett given the boot. Lincoln-Mercury created.

1947 Henry Ford dies at age 83. Chuck Yeager's Bell X-1 aircraft breaks sound barrier.

1938 Henry Ford suffers stroke in his 75th year.

1946 Henry Ford II begins hiring his "Whiz Kids," a group of young executives who almost instantly revitalize the aging firm. Former GM exec Ernest Breech hired as Ford vice president.

Brand Ne
FOR

1940 Edsel Ford's classic Lincoln Continental debuts. Movie *Gone With The Wind* wins Academy Award.

1942 Production of cars and trucks for civilian use suspended to allow automotive industry to concentrate on war effort.

1944 "Cast-Iron Charlie" Sorenson quits Ford.

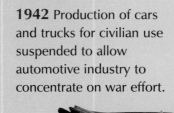

1943 Edsel Ford dies. Henry Ford returns to president's chair. Henry Ford II released from military service to hopefully take control of company.

ABOVE: *1949 Lincoln Junior convertible.*

1948 F-series truck lin introduced. Polaroid Land Camera goes on sale. GM introduces au industry's first modern overhead-valve, short-stroke, high-compression V8.

1941 Japanese attack on Pearl Harbor and draws America into World War II. Henry Ford II goes into U.S. Navy.

1939 Ford finally introduces hydraulic brakes. Mid-priced Mercury line debuts. Germany invades Poland.

1949 All-new postwar Lincoln, Mercury and Ford models introduced as profits soar to $177 million. Ford Division officially established.

1951 First optional automatic transmission debuts for Ford cars. Ford Archives established in preparation for 50th anniversary celebration.

1953 Ford Motor Company celebrates its 50th anniversary. A Ford convertible leads the pace lap for the Indianapolis 500. Milestone F-100 pickup truck introduced

1956 Henry Ford II puts Ford stock back up for public sale for first time in 37 years. *Motor Trend* magazine extends its "Car of the Year honors to entire Ford model line.

1958 National recession hits all American carmakers hard. Redesigned four-place Thunderbird earns *Motor Trend*'s "Car of the Year" award. Edsel debacle begins in earnest.

1959 Import car sales reach record heights in America. Ford Credit, Detroit's largest auto leasing company, is established.

ABOVE RIGHT: *1953 Lincoln Capri convertible coupe.*

1955 Ford established profit record at $437 million. Ford production, at 1.4 million, is second best ever. "Whiz Kid" Robert McNamara becomes Ford general manager.

1954 Henry Ford's venerable "flathead" V8 replaced by the new overhead-valve V8 known as the "Y-block." Ford becomes first low-priced car to replace obsolete kingpins in front suspension with modern ball joints. Ford's magical Thunderbird debuts as 1955 model.

1957 Baseball's Brooklyn Dodgers leave New York for Los Angeles. Half-car/half-truck Ranchero introduced by Ford. Ford builds last two-seat T-bird—for now. Mercury Turnpike Cruiser paces Indy 500.

1952 New Lincolns debut with Ford Motor Company's first overhead-valve V8 engine.

BELOW: *1957 Ranchero Custom Pickup truck.*

RUCKS
BUILT STRONGER TO LAST LONGER

1950 Clara Ford dies, also at age 83. "Police action" in Korea begins. Minimum wage of 75 cents an hour goes into effect.

1960   **1961**   **1962**   **1963**   **1964**   **1965**   **1966**   **1967**   **1968**   **1969**   **197**

1961 Ford tops Chevrolet in annual sales race. Alan Shepard, Jr., becomes first American in space.

1962 Ford introduces its first mid-sized model, Fairlane. Carroll Shelby begins building Ford-powered Cobra in Southern California.

1963 Thunderbird Sports Roadster

1965 Carroll Shelby introduces his GT-350 Shelby Mustang. "Twin I-Beam" suspension introduced for Ford trucks. First official U.S. combat forces land in South Vietnam.

1969 Ford intro compact Maveri 1970 model. GT collects fourth consecutive vict Le Mans. Henry fires Bunkie Knu Neil Armstrong becomes first m the moon.

1968 Former GM exec Semon E. "Bunkie" Knudsen hired as Ford president. "Ford has a better idea" advertising slogan first heard.

1960 Ford's new compact, Falcon, establishes Detroit record for first-year new-model sales. Robert McNamara succeeds Henry II as president but leaves after one month to become President John Kennedy's Secretary of Defense. Lee Iacocca becomes Ford general manager. Edsel cancelled.

ABOVE: *1964 Mustang*

1964 Ford Mustang ushers in "ponycar" era. Mustang convertible paces Indy 500. "British invasion" begins as Beatles arrive at New York's Kennedy Airport.

1963 President John F. Kenneday assassinated in Dallas, Texas. "Whiz Kid" Arjay Miller replaces John Dykstra to become the seventh president in Ford history. Henry Ford II attempts to buy Ferrari but fails.

1967 Ford of Europe formed. Biggest Thunderbird yet appears, including four-door version. Three American astronauts killed in fire during test of Apollo spacecraft in Florida.

BELOW: *1966 GT40*

1966 Ford's GT40 race cars finish 1-2-3 at legendary 24 Hours of Le Mans. Ford builds one millionth Mustang. Henry Ford II divorces his wife and marries Italian socialite.

1970 Henry Ford II shuts down nearly all racing projects. Lee Iacocca becomes Ford president.

| 1971 | 1972 | 1973 | 1974 | 1975 | 1976 | 1977 | 1978 | 1979 | 1980 | 1981 |

ABOVE: *The Ranchero and allied utilities.*

1977 Ford truck sales hit record high at 1.2 million.

1978 Ford celebrates its 75th anniversary. Henry Ford II fires Lee Iacocca. Iacocca then heads straight for Chrysler.

1980 Ford records incredible $1.54 billion loss. Jack Telnack rises to top of Ford styling department. Special Vehicle Operations (SVO) formed.

1975 U.S. involvement in Vietnam War ends. Television viewers convinced by ads that new Ford Granada could be mistaken for Mercedes.

LEFT: *1973 Capri*

ABOVE: *1974 Mustang II hatchback coupe.*

1979 Redesigned Fox-chassis Mustang paces Indy 500. Ford acquires 25 per cent interest in Mazda.

1971 Longer, heavier, more expensive Mustang debuts. Charles Manson and others convicted in grisly murder of actress Sharon Tate and six others.

1974 Smaller, lighter, more affordable Mustang II debuts. U.S. president Richard Nixon resigns in wake of Watergate scandal.

1972 Henry Ford II and architect John Portman announce plans to rebuild downtown Detroit; construction of Renaissance Center follows.

RIGHT: *1979 Mustang Indy Pace Car Replica.*

1973 Energy crisis results after Organization of Petroleum Exporting Countries (OPEC) cut back oil delivered to West in protest of U.S. support of Israel.

1976 Americans celebrate bicentennial.

1981 Japan automakers agree to limit exports from across the Pacific. Ford's losses for year reach $1.06 billion.

1982 **1983** **1984** **1985** **1986** **1987** **1988** **1989** **1990** **1991** **199**

1982 Henry Ford II retires. Space shuttle flights begin as Columbia launches successfully.

1984 Ford profit reaches record high of $2.91 billion.

1986 Taurus earns *Motor Trend*'s "Car of the Year" trophy. Ford acquires 10 per cent interest in Kia Motor Company of South Korea.

1989 Thunderbird named *Motor Trend*'s "Car of the Year" for the second time in three years. William Clay Ford, Sr., retires as vice president making this the first time that no one named Ford will hold top management spot.

ABOVE: *1989 Mustang LX convertible.*

1987 Henry Ford II dies of pneumonia. Ford sets new profits record at $4.63 billion. Ford buys 75 per cent interest in Aston Martin Lagonda, Ltd., of England.

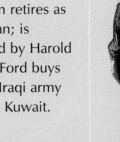

ABOVE: *'65 and '89 Mustangs.*

1990 Donald Petersen retires as chairman; is replaced by Harold Poling. Ford buys Jaguar. Iraqi army invades Kuwait.

1991 Ford's Explorer explodes on the scene to dominate early SUV sales. U.S. forces defeat Iraq in Persian Gulf War.

RIGHT: *1989 Probe coupe*

ABOVE: *1986 SVO mustang*

1983 Popular television show *M*A*S*H* runs final episode.

1985 Donald Petersen becomes Ford chairman; Harold Poling becomes Ford president. Ford Taurus introduced as 1986 model. Rock and Roll Hall of Fame announced.

1988 Both Edsel Ford II and William Clay Ford, Jr., gain board of directors positions. Ford buys 80 per cent interest in Hertz Rent-A-Car.

1992 F-series pickup is America's best-selling vehicle for 10th straigh year. Hurricane Andrew strongest ever to strike U.S., sweeps across southern Florida.

Ford

| 993 | 1994 | 1995 | 1996 | 1997 | 1998 | 1999 | 2000 | 2001 | 2002 | 2003 |

1995 "Ford 2000" restructuring program initiated to better organize global affairs in preparation for doing business in the new millennium to come.

BELOW, RIGHT: *1996 Taurus LX station wagon.*

2001 World Trade Center towers in New York toppled after terrorist attacks. U.S. and allied forces strike back at Afghanistan's Taliban regime.

2002 New GT40 debuts at Detroit Auto Show. Ford's "No Boundaries" advertising campaign begins.

1997 Ford kills off traditional two-door Thunderbird coupe.

1998 Four-door Taurus selected to replace Thunderbird on NASCAR racing circuit.

2000 William Clay Ford, Jr., becomes Ford CEO.

BELOW: *2003 GT40*

ABOVE: *1996 Mustang GT convertible coupe.*

Atlanta Assembly Plant
6 MILLIONTH TAURUS SOLD!

1993 Englishman Alex Trotman becomes chairman and CEO of Ford Motor Company. Five of America's top eight best-selling vehicles are Fords.

1996 Ford of Korea formed as joint venture with Kia.

1994 SVT Cobra Mustang convertible paces Indy 500.

1999 William Clay Ford, Jr., elected chairman of board. Ford buys Volvo. New two-seat Thunderbird concept car debuts at Detroit Auto Show.

2003 Ford Motor Company celebrates is 100th anniversary, as does Buick. Space shuttle Columbia disintegrates upon re-entry from earth orbit.

ABOVE: *2003 GT40 - and the road goes on forever....*

Picture Credits
All pictures copyright © Mike Mueller except for the following:

Chrysalis Images
51, 64, 102-3, 116-7, 120-1, 136-7, 134-5, 140-1, 142-3, 150-1

Andrew Moreland
27 top & bottom, 34

Detroit Public Library
22-3